Introducing . . .

S0-BJG-214

PROPHECY IN THE RING

Prophecy is one of the most vibrant subjects of Scripture and many fine books have been written on it. But never one on prophecy in the ring. What do we mean by this term? Evangelical theologians and students of Scripture have long held tenaciously to particular views of future happenings. Much time and effort are spent in defense of the various views. The result is that evangelicals, who otherwise have so much in common, fiercely battle each other in less than Christian ways. And there is no question about it, prophecy is in the ring.

Why? We are going to find out in this study. We will try to discover a way for God's people to hang up the gloves. Convictions? Yes, but let's speak the truth in love.

PROPHECY IN THE RING

ROBERT P. LIGHTNER

G. Allen Fleece Library
Columbia International University
Columbia, SC 29203

ACCENT BOOKS
Denver, Colorado

MEMBER OF
EVANGELICAL CHRISTIAN
PUBLISHERS ASSOCIATION

All rights reserved. No portion of this book may be reproduced in any form without the written permission of the publishers, with the exception of brief excerpts in magazine reviews.

Accent Publications
12100 W. Sixth Avenue
P.O. Box 15337
Denver, Colorado 80215

Copyright © 1976 B/P Publications, Inc.
Printed in U.S.A.

Library of Congress Catalog Card Number: 76-8736
ISBN 0-916406-21-0

Contents

Charts and Diagrams

Acknowledgments

I owe much to many who assisted me in different ways in the preparation of this book.

A special word of thanks to my wife, Pearl, who labored long and hard typing the manuscript in the midst of her many other duties. She has learned well how to read my handwritten scribble.

For help on the title and editorial assistance I am indebted to my good friend Howard Laing.

Many others have helped me in many ways, some through their publications and others through personal conversations and dialogue.

I also wish to express my gratitude to Dallas Theological Seminary for extending to me a semester's leave of absence from my seminary duties to do this and other research projects. Discussion with my colleagues has been most rewarding and helpful.

CHAPTER 1

Why Another Book About the Future?

Why another book about the future? Isn't it time for a halt to the flood of material dealing with prophecy? It would seem so. But this is a different kind of book on prophecy. It is a book that should have been written long ago.

The Bible is an inspired record about what happened many years ago. Much of both the Old and New Testaments is history. By no means, however, does it record only what took place in the past. Much of the content of God's inerrant Word is about future events. Unfulfilled prophecy forms a vital part of holy Scripture. This book is concerned with the Bible's unfulfilled prophecies and with the conflict among evangelicals over the meaning and fulfillment of those prophecies.

THE TERMS DEFINED

A word of orientation and background will help us. Just as there are liberals and conservatives in the political world, so there are the same in the religious world. There are also variations of these two groupings, both in politics and religion. For example, there are extreme liberals and moderate liberals, just as there are strong conservatives and moderate conservatives. Other descriptions abound, such as right and left wing.

In many instances the label one is given or the position he is said to embrace is a subjective thing. We often set ourselves up as the standard of judgment. Too many times we define the center, the true view, as we want to and then assign others accordingly—left or right of us.

In 1909 two Christian laymen made possible the publication of a twelve volume set called *The Fundamentals*.[1] Some three million copies of this scholarly defense of the faith were circulated. This monumental work restated and clearly defined Biblical and historic Christianity. The contributors were men of great scholarship and faith. The work was a defense of the faith against the attacks which had been made upon it by secular philosophy, unbelieving science, and modern or liberal theology.

Five major doctrines, and themes related to them, were set forth. The doctrines were the following:

1. The inspiration and authority of Scripture

2. The virgin birth of Christ

3. The deity of Christ

4. The substitutionary atonement of Christ

5. The bodily resurrection of Christ and His second coming

A quick look at the list tells us that the two doctrines around which the others revolved were the Person and work of Christ and the inspiration of the Bible.

On the basis of these fundamentals, the fundamentalists and the liberals, or modernists as they were called then, were separated. The lines were clearly drawn. Those who embraced these great doctrines of the faith were called fundamentalists and those who did not were called modernists.

Today other terms are sometimes used to designate these two groups. Modernists are called liberals and fundamentalists are sometimes called evangelicals. Actually, the word *evangelical* is a Biblical one and when used in its historic sense, describes those who with conviction believe the five fundamentals of the faith.

As is the case with most words, *evangelical* and *evangelicalism* have been given new meanings and need to be explained, but so do the words *fundamental* and *fundamentalism*, for that matter. They too are sometimes used today to represent more than belief in the five fundamentals of the faith. Descriptive words like these all have overtones or connotations which are undesirable.

When I use the term *evangelical* or *evangelicalism* in this book, I am referring to one who accepts the five fundamentals of the faith. The term designates one who is orthodox in his beliefs in contrast to one who is unorthodox.

This study will deal with only one of the five fundamentals. While all who are legitimately called evangelical or fundamental believe all five, there are considerable differences in the ranks over how to understand some of the details concerning the second coming of Christ.

He will return! Evangelicals agree fully on that. On the questions of what specifics will be included, what the exact order of events will be, and in what sequence of time they will come to pass, however, there is by no means complete agreement.

THE HISTORICAL SETTING

Many Christians consider all the fuss about future things unnecessary. They view the discussion as inconsequential and a big waste of time and effort. As far as they are concerned, it is more important that we get out the gospel than it is to debate what they consider to be trivialities about how events will unfold in the future.

On the other hand, theologians and students of Scripture hold tenaciously to particular views of future happenings. Denominations, mission agencies, schools, and other Christian organizations, as well as individuals, are divided over God's plan for the future. Much time and effort are spent in defense of the various views. Why? Prophecy is in the ring all right. I doubt that very many would deny that. But the question remains. Why? We are going to try to find out why in this study.

Rightly or wrongly, the evangelical world is divided over the order of things to come. Needless to say, that is an understatement. What is more, the division has existed for a long time. Since the third century of the Christian era, the controversy has raged. In the last 150 or 200 years it has been serious. But in the last 15 or 20 years the conflict has increased to the point of crisis.

A notable theologian with a special interest in the subject of prophecy and future things made this observation regarding the renewed interest in the question of future events. "The events of the last quarter of a century or more have had a tremendous impact on the thinking of the scholarly world. In philosophy there has been a trend toward realism and increasing interest in ultimate values and ethics. In science, the moral significance of scientific knowledge and the growing realization that physical science is a part of world life and meaning have emerged. In theology, there has been what amounts to a similar revolution, particularly in the study of prophecy."[2]

Equally dedicated, sincere, and godly men have contended for one of three major views regarding God's program for the future. *Premillennialism* is the view that Christ will return and institute on earth a kingdom of perfect peace and righteousness 1000 years in duration. After this time eternity begins. *Amillennialism* is the view that when Christ returns, eternity begins with no millennial reign on earth before. The *postmillennial* view (not very common at the present) has it that through the church's influence the world will be Christianized before Christ returns. Immediately following His return eternity begins. Each of these views will be explained further in Chapter 4.

One thing is sure, these three schools of thought cannot all be right. The views cancel out each other. I suspect that a good number of Christians would not be disappointed if all three views would be canceled out and that the tug of war among Christians over prophecy would cease. No doubt, many would like to call for a moratorium on the prophecy debate. For them, that would be the coming of the kingdom.

But the war won't stop, though a better understanding of the reasons for the conflict will lessen the tension. The differences will probably prevail until the Lord Himself comes and fulfills His Word. So let's not engage ourselves in wishful thinking. Let's face the facts and tell it like it is. It is about time we took a long, careful look at the various views of the future and their relation to God's Word. Also, it is essential that we see the importance of unfulfilled prophecy and its relationship to other areas of the Bible's teaching.

Unfortunately, the three views of the future defined above have often been set forth as primarily the result of one's interpretation of the references to the "one thousand years" in Revelation 20:1-7. I do not think that is the case. Instead of one's interpretation of this phrase determining his millennial view, it is the other way around. One's millennial system arrived at on other Biblical grounds will determine how he will interpret Revelation 20:1-7.

Scriptural teaching of the millennium or kingdom is by no means confined to specific kingdom terminology. One who could not be classified as a special friend of evangelicalism made this point with real force: "For the concept of the Kingdom of God involves in a real sense the total message of the Bible. Not only does it loom large in the teachings, it is to be found in one form or

another through the length and breadth of the Bible . . . .
Old Testament and New Testament thus stand together as
the two acts of a single drama. Act I points to its
conclusion in Act II, and without it the play is an
incomplete unsatisfying thing. But Act II must be read in
the light of Act I else its meaning would be missed. Where
the play is organically one, the Bible is one Book. Had we
to give that book a title, we might with justice call it, The
Book of the Coming Kingdom of God."[3]

A CALL TO CONSIDER

It is my desire that this book will contribute to the
reduction of the warfare among evangelicals over the
understanding of unfulfilled prophecies. I have not
written to stir up more controversy or to enlarge the
battle over future things. I am convinced there is a good
deal of misunderstanding and misrepresentation in the
furor over the future. No doubt, much of this is because
of insufficient information or misdirected zeal, or maybe
some of both.

Those who know me, especially those who have sat
under my teaching and preaching, know that I have
definite views regarding things to come. I think
everybody should. But it is not my purpose in these pages
to set forth or to defend my own views. This book is not
a defense of any particular view of future events. Neither
is it my purpose to make the positions I do not agree
with look bad and to make those who hold them look
ignorant.

I am not so naive as to believe that this volume will
serve to solve all the problems, eliminate all the
differences, and bring about a cessation of the war over
eschatology among evangelicals. And I should emphasize
that I will be dealing only with the views of evangelicals
in these pages. The book is designed, however, to provide
those in the pew as well as those in the pulpit with a
better understanding of their own views and why

14

Christians differ over these matters. With this understanding I hope there will also come a deeper commitment to the Lord Jesus Christ, the Living Word of God, and the Bible, the written Word of God. When this is realized, there will be a deeper love for the people of God regardless of their understanding of things to come.

Several positive reasons prompt me to write this volume. First, I want to set forth the various views held by evangelicals with regard to the future. Second, the reasons for their differences need to be explored and explained. Third, I want to alert the Christian public concerning the intensity of the battle over the Bible's teaching about things to come. Most clergymen and church leaders know about the conflict, but many laymen do not. They have a right to know why men of God who agree on all the essentials or fundamentals of the faith differ so widely and battle so tenaciously over prophecy. Why fight over things to come, anyway? What makes this doctrine so different from the others over which Christians have differences? These are basic questions of this study.

Fourth, I want to suggest that evangelicals begin to practice in their views of prophecy what they preach in their doctrine of the family of God. It is time that we start behaving like brothers and sisters in the heavenly family. Each child in the household of faith is needed. We must never forget that. The exercise of Christian love is just as essential in eschatology as it is in every other area of God's truth.

If what I have said here makes even the smallest contribution toward the easing of tensions over things to come, it will have been well worth the effort. May God grant it is my prayer.

NOTES FOR CHAPTER 1

[1]The Fundamentals—A Testimony to the Truth (Chicago: Testimony Publishing Company, 1909).

[2]John F. Walvoord, *The Millennial Kingdom* (Findlay, Ohio: Dunham Publishing Company, 1959), p. 3.

[3]John Bright, *The Kingdom of God* (Nashville: Abingdon, 1953), pp. 1,7,197.

CHAPTER 2

Evangelical Agreement on Major Unfulfilled Prophecies

From beginning to end the Bible is filled with prophecy. Someone has said that one-fourth of all the books of the Bible are prophetic in nature and one-fifth of the actual text of Scripture was prophetic when it was written. [1] Whether or not these percentages are altogether accurate may be debated by some. It must be admitted, though, that Scripture abounds with prophecy. Much of what has been predicted in the Bible has already come to pass.

Perhaps the best example of fulfilled prophecies are those related to the Lord Jesus Christ. Over 300 prophecies were fulfilled at the first advent of Christ. An example of some of these related to His earthly ministry and sacrificial death are included in the charts,[2] *Christ's Ministry Predicted* and *Christ's Death Predicted.*

Christ's Ministry Predicted

Element of Christ's Ministry	Old Testament Prediction	New Testament Fulfillment
Location	Isaiah 9:1,2	Matthew 4:13-16
Power	Isaiah 11:2	Luke 3:22; 4:1
Saving Character	Isaiah 61:1	Luke 4:16-19
Healing Character	Isaiah 53:4	Matthew 8:16,17
Miracles	Isaiah 35:5,6	Matthew 11:4,5
Inclusion of Gentiles	Isaiah 42:1,6	Luke 2:32
Zeal	Psalm 69:9	John 2:17
Serving Character	Isaiah 42:1-4	Matthew 12:15-21
Humility	Zechariah 9:9	Matthew 21:4,5
Rejection	Isaiah 53:3	John 1:11

Christ's Death Predicted

Event of the Passion	Old Testament Prediction	New Testament Fulfillment
To be deserted	Zechariah 13:7	Matthew 26:31

18

To be scourged and spat on	Isaiah 50:6	Matthew 26:67
To be given vinegar to drink	Psalm 69:21	Matthew 27:34,48
To be pierced with nails	Psalm 22:16	Luke 23:33
To be forsaken by God	Psalm 22:1	Matthew 27:46
To be surrounded by enemies	Isaiah 22:7,8	Matthew 27:39,40
To be numbered with transgressors	Isaiah 53:12	Mark 15:28
To agonize with thirst	Psalm 22:15	John 19:28
To commend His spirit to God	Psalm 31:5	Luke 23:46
To have His garments distributed	Psalm 22:18	John 19:23,24
To have no bone broken	Psalm 34:20	John 19:33-36
To be buried with the rich	Isaiah 53:9	Matthew 27:57-60
To rise from the dead	Psalm 16:9,10	Acts 2:27,31
To ascend into glory	Psalm 68:18	Ephesians 4:8

There are a significant number of predictions made in the Bible which have not yet come to pass. Regardless what view one takes of the order or manner in which these are to be fulfilled, all who accept the Bible as God's infallible Word agree they have not yet been fulfilled but will be in the future.

The order in which these major unfulfilled prophecies are presented is not significant. In fact, I have purposely tried to avoid any order which would reveal my own view of the future order of events. My purpose is not to defend any particular scheme of prophecy. Evangelicals agree there is unfulfilled prophecy; that is what I want to emphasize here. Those who love the Lord and His Word have little argument with each other about the certainty of these future events. What they do argue about, sometimes in very unchristian ways, is the order in which these things will be fulfilled, the time sequence. Boxing is not the only thing in the ring. Unfortunately, Christians in their interpretation of details of prophecy concerning the future are too!

Our primary concern, however, in this chapter will be with those prophecies of Scripture which all evangelicals agree have not been fulfilled to this time. In other words, we want to know what are the major unfulfilled prophecies, the things still to come, over which evangelicals do not fight. What subjects of prophecy are not in the ring?

THE ETERNAL STATE

Heaven is a real place of habitation. So is hell. Human beings will spend eternity in one or the other of these places. The Bible plainly says both places exist and will be occupied by human souls forever.

Critical Biblical scholarship tells us we can no longer believe the pre-Copernican view of the universe. Science, we are told, has disproved belief in a three-decker universe which was a common belief about the time the

Bible was being written. The sun, not the earth, is the center of everything, modern science insists. Therefore, up is no longer really up, for earth dwellers, and down is no longer down.

Such views were bound to make an impact upon theological thinking sooner or later. And they did. Rudolph Bultmann expressed his unbelief in the Bible's view of heaven and hell this way: "Man's knowledge and mastery of the world have advanced to such an extent through science and technology that it is no longer possible for anyone seriously to hold the New Testament view of the world—in fact, there is no one who does . . . No one who is old enough to think for himself supposes that God lives in a local heaven. There is no longer any heaven in the traditional sense of the word. The same applies to hell in the sense of a mythical under-world beneath our feet. And if this is so, we can no longer accept the story of Christ's descent into hell or his Ascension into heaven as literally true. We can no longer look for the return of the Son of Man on the clouds of heaven or hope that the faithful will meet him in the air (I Thess. 4:15ff)."[3]

As far as most of modern science is concerned, truth does not exist outside the scientific realm. The supernatural, the miraculous, is denied by unbelieving scientists and consequently by much of modern theology as well.

In response to the contention that we can no longer accept the Bible's teaching about heaven and hell being real places and remain intellectually honest Leslie Woodson said, "What is so often overlooked is that there are different truth dimensions and truth in one of these dimensions need not be denied by truth in another. Their natures are not the same. Thus, one can be intellectually honest while embracing both a Copernican view of the physcial world and a three-decker view of the metaphysical world at one and the same time."[4]

Time will not go on forever! There can be no debate about that among Bible believers. Eternity is as much a future certainty as time is a present reality. If the Bible doesn't teach that, it doesn't teach anything.

When will time end and eternity begin? That is another question. But that there is a future world out there is not disputed by God's people. No believing student of the Bible accepts the notion that death ends it all.

The true Biblical teaching of both heaven and hell is often neglected today. It is also often misrepresented. Modern man uses the Biblical terminology but invests it with new meaning. For example, experience of a hard life are sometimes described as "hell on earth." The person who is deprived of the good things or even the essential things of life is said to be "going through hell." Ron Devillier gave this description of hell: "Hell is where the poor are trapped in a ghetto of indifference. It is the high school campus where some persons are socially crippled because they don't fit. It is the black section of a psychiatric ward at a charity hospital where the bruised ones that didn't get enough love are hidden. It is a small village in Vietnam where people lie in the streets, victims of a stray bomb. It is a dingy jail downtown where frightened human beings cower. It is a small town high school where a teenage girl returns from a home for unwed mothers after giving birth to her child. It is the street of charred buildings, broken windows, and looted stores—the aftermath of a riot kindled by frustration, hopelessness, and rage."[5]

The one who wrote the above may have a Biblical view of hell all right but his words in this instance do not reveal it. To be sure, those who go through the experiences he described are having the nearest thing to "hell on earth." But the Bible would have us understand that there is a hell far worse than anything possible on this earth. No amount of misfortune and poverty with all that goes with them even begins to compare with the horrors and torments of hell. Those who reject the Lord Jesus Christ as their Saviour will go to a place of eternal torment which the Bible calls the lake of fire.

Evangelicals believe in an eternal existence for man either in heaven or hell because the Bible teaches it. Prophecy concerning man's existence in these two abodes is not in the ring.

Concerning heaven Jesus said to His own, "I go to prepare a place for you" (John 14:2). Where He would be, He said, He wanted them also (verse 3).

Hell, Jesus taught, was also a place of eternal torment for the devil, his angels, and sons and daughters of Adam who rejected Him and His sacrifice for their sins. A place of "damnation" where "the fire is not quenched," He called it (Matthew 23:33; Mark 9:48).

In addition, of course, to what Jesus said about heaven and hell as eternal abodes there is an abundance of other Scripture teaching the same thing.

Evangelicals agree too that there will be a new heaven and a new earth in the future. The prophet Isaiah wrote of these. He recorded Jehovah's answer to the prayer of the believing remnant. In part, the answer was, "Behold, I create new heavens and a new earth, and the former shall not be remembered, nor come into mind" (Isaiah 65:17). "For as the new heaven and the new earth, which I will make, shall remain before men, saith the LORD, so shall your seed and your name remain" (Isaiah 66:22).

In New Testament times Peter was still predicting judgment upon the "heavens and the earth which are now" (II Peter 3:7). He said also, "The heavens shall pass away with a great noise, and the elements shall melt with fervent heat; the earth also, and the works that are in it, shall be burned up" (verse 10). But, he prophesied further, we "look for new heavens and a new earth, in which dwelleth righteousness" (verse 13).

John in his apocalyptic vision saw Christ on a throne and from his "face the earth and the heaven fled away"

(Revelation 20:11). Also, the beloved disciple "saw a new heaven and a new earth" (Revelation 21:1).

The present heavens and earth have not yet been "destroyed." The prophecy that they will awaits future fulfillment. And so does the prophecy of the creation of a new heaven and earth. Bible believers do not differ on these things. They agree that the eternal state has not yet begun.

FUTURE DIVINE JUDGMENT

Nonevangelicals find it impossible to reconcile the doctrine of divine judgment with their concept of God. And that is understandable since they reject so much of what the Bible says about God.

Any concept of God as heavenly Father which likens Him to a soft, lenient, permissive, earthly father is not true to the Biblical representation of Him. He is love, indeed; He is not a tyrant who rejoices in His judgment and punishment for sin. But God is righteous and just, too, and His love moved Him to make provision for sin in His Son. Rejection of Christ, His Son, means rejection of the only acceptable remedy for sin. Righteous wrath awaits all who reject God's Son as personal Saviour!

That all men, as well as Satan and all the wicked angels, will one day stand before the God of the Bible in judgment is universally accepted by those who accept the Bible as God's Word. Conflict does not exist among evangelicals over this unfulfilled prophecy.

The question among Christians is not, Will God bring all to judgment? They all agree, He will. Will all be judged at the same time? That is, will the unsaved, the saved, and Satan and all his angels all appear before God together at the same time? On that question there is a great deal of difference.

But right now we are not concerned with the differences among evangelicals. The broad area of agreement is what we want to explore.

The agreement among evangelicals of the certainty of future divine judgment is not marred by their differences over the order of events. Their high view of God and His Word brings them all to the conclusion that divine judgment is ahead. True, God does judge sin in the present. Yet Scripture makes clear that these judgments of God experienced in the here and now are not final.

From the very beginning of the Christian era belief in future divine judgment was associated with belief in the certainty of the future resurrection of all men. The dead are to be raised so that they might be judged. The Apostle's Creed, earliest apostolic testimony about Christ, puts it succinctly when it states that Christ "shall come to judge the quick and the dead."

That all the unregenerate will one day appear before God in judgment is clear from John's record of the revelation God gave him: "And I saw a great white throne, and him that sat on it, from whose face the earth and the heaven fled away, and there was found no place for them. And I saw the dead, small and great, stand before God, and the books were opened; and another book was opened, which is the book of life. And the dead were judged out of those things which were written in the books, according to their works. And the sea gave up the dead that were in it, and death and hades delivered up the dead that were in them; and they were judged every man according to their works. And death and hades were cast into the lake of fire. This is the second death. And whosoever was not found written in the book of life was cast into the lake of fire" (Revelation 20:11-15).

Scripture is equally as clear in its prophecy of the certainty of believers standing personally before God in the future to give an account to Him. The apostle Paul reminded the Christians in Corinth and in Rome of this.

To the Corinthians he wrote: "Every man's work shall be made manifest; for the day shall declare it, because it shall be revealed by fire; and the fire shall test every man's work of what sort it is. If any man's work abide which he hath built upon it, he shall receive a reward. If any man's work shall be burned, he shall suffer loss; but he himself shall be saved, yet as by fire" (I Corinthians 3:13-15).

In his second letter to the same people he wrote, "For we must all appear before the judgment seat of Christ, that everyone may receive the things done in his body, according to that he hath done, whether it be good or bad" (II Corinthians 5:10).

The Roman Christians were given the very same teaching: "But why dost thou judge thy brother? Or why dost thou set at nought thy brother? For we shall all stand before the judgment seat of Christ. For it is written, As I live saith the Lord, every knee shall bow to me, and every tongue shall confess to God. So then, every one of us shall give account of himself to God" (Romans 14:10-12).

Final judgment also awaits the devil and his demons. The everlasting fire of hell was prepared for the devil and his angels (Matthew 25:41). In his vision John was given to see "the devil that deceived them . . . cast into the lake of fire and brimstone, where the beast and the false prophet are." There he is to be tormented day and night for ever and ever (Revelation 20:10).

Peter and Jude both were directed by the Holy Spirit to tell us of wicked angels being reserved in chains until the day of their final judgment (II Peter 2:4; Jude 1:6).

Without regard to denominational affiliation or lack of it and no matter whether one believes there will be one final judgment or whether there will be a number of different judgments separated by time, all evangelicals believe in a future divine judgment. They take the words of the Psalmist seriously and as yet unfulfilled when he said: "Before the LORD; for he cometh, for he cometh to judge the earth; he shall judge the world with righteousness, and the peoples with his truth" (Psalm 96:13).

FUTURE BODILY RESURRECTION

It has always been true. It was true when Jesus was on earth; some believed in the resurrection and others did not. The Pharisees accepted the doctrine but the Sadducees rejected it (Matthew 22:23; Acts 23:8). Their differences over the resurrection did not, of course, keep them from joining together in their opposition to the Saviour. They were perfectly willing to overlook their differences so they could form a united front against Christ.

When Paul preached the doctrine of the resurrection on Mars' Hill he was met with mocking and scoffing (Acts 17:32). There were others in New Testament times who either doubted the doctrine or regarded the resurrection as purely spiritual (I Corinthians 15:12; II Timothy 2:18).

Evangelicals base their view of future resurrection upon the clear teaching of Scripture.

They see implications and direct teaching of the doctrine in the Old Testament (Psalm 49:15; 73:24,25; Proverbs 23:14; Job 19:25-27; Isaiah 26:19; Daniel 12:2).

In the New Testament there is even more teaching about the future resurrection of the dead. Jesus Himself argued for the resurrection in opposition to the Sadducees (Matthew 22:23-33). As He did so He paralleled what He said with what the Old Testament said in Genesis 17:7; 26:24; 28:21 and Exodus 3:6. He appealed to these texts in defense of His teaching (cf. Matthew 22:31,32).

On another occasion in reply to His critics Jesus set forth the doctrine of future resurrection for the dead. He said, ". . . the hour is coming, in which all that are in the graves shall hear his voice, And shall come forth: they that have done good, unto the resurrection of life; and they that have done evil, unto the resurrection of damnation" (John 5:28,29).

Repeatedly Jesus promised to "raise up at the last day" those who belonged to Him (John 6:39,40,44,54). He claimed to be the "resurrection and the life" (John 11:24,25).

On the basis of these and other clear passages of Scripture there is common agreement among evangelicals —all the dead will be raised at God's appointed time in the future. Again, regardless of other differences, all who name the name of Christ in truth can repeat the Apostle's Creed without tongue in cheek when it says, "I believe in The Resurrection of the body."

FUTURE RETURN OF CHRIST

The Old Testament prophets did not distinguish between Christ's coming as a babe in Bethlehem's manger and His coming the second time in power and great glory.

What they prophesied concerning Christ's return is understood differently by evangelicals. Some see all the Old Testament prophecies of Christ's coming as already fulfilled at His first advent. Others believe a significant number of the prophecies await future fulfillment when He comes again.

Nevertheless, all Bible believers do agree that in the New Testament we have clear prophecy of Christ's coming to the earth again. Jesus and the writers of the New Testament agree, His first coming will be followed by a second one.

Those who witnessed Jesus's ascension heard the angelic messengers say, "Ye men of Galilee, why stand ye gazing up into heaven? This same Jesus, who is taken up from you into heaven, shall so come in like manner as ye have seen him go into heaven" (Acts 1:11).

Long before He returned to the Father, Jesus taught His own that He would come again. On one occasion as He sat on the Mount of Olives, He told His disciples about the future. They were warned of difficult times ahead and were assured of their Lord's return. "For then shall be great tribulation, such as was not since the beginning of the world to this time, no, nor ever shall be. And except those days should be shortened, there should no flesh be saved; but for the elect's sake those days shall be shortened. Then if any man shall say unto you, Lo, here is Christ, or there; believe it nor. For there shall arise false Christs and false prophets, and shall show great signs and wonders, insomuch that, if it were possible, they shall deceive the very elect. Behold, I have told you before. Wherefore, if they shall say unto you, Behold, he is in the desert; go not forth; behold, he is in the secret chambers. believe it not. For as the lightning cometh out of the east, and shineth even unto the west, so shall also the coming of the Son of man be" (Matthew 24:21-27).

In what has come to be called Christ's Upper Room Discourse He brought comfort to His disciples by announcing that He would come again for them. They did not want to think about His death. "I will come again, and receive you unto myself," Jesus assured them (John 14:3).

The very last book in the Bible still holds out the promise of Christ's second coming. John, in vision, saw Christ, "The Word of God," coming from heaven to the earth along with the armies of heaven (Revelation 19:11-16).

Evangelicals do not fight over these prophecies. They all agree they have not yet been fulfilled. Will Christ come first in the air for all His children (I Thessalonians 4:13-18)? Is this coming to be distinguished from His coming to the earth (Revelation 19:11-16). Evangelicals answer differently to such questions. But they do all concur—Christ is coming to the earth again just as surely as He came the first time.

So, what have we discovered thus far in our study? We have seen that despite differences over details evangelicals agree on several major issues regarding prophecy of things to come. They agree man lives on after death. Heaven as well as hell will be occupied by people. There will be a new heaven and a new earth in the future. All of God's creatures will face Him in future judgment. The dead, small and great, will be raised to spend eternity either with God in heaven or with the devil in hell. Christ is coming back to this earth again. His coming will be just as literal as when He came as a babe in Bethlehem's manger.

We evangelicals have so much in common. The great fundamentals of the faith bind us together in the family of God. One of those fundamentals is the doctrine of the future bodily return of Christ. Fellowship in the things of the Lord which we hold in common rather than fighting over details of unfulfilled prophecy should characterize our lives.

In the next chapter we will present the different evangelical viewpoints with regard to how and in what order these future happenings will take place. There are a number of variations of the time sequence and the details accompanying these major unfulfilled prophecies. Study of these will get us close to the ring where there is fighting, some of it fierce and without regard to any rules.

[1] Lewis Sperry Chafer, *Systematic Theology* (Dallas: Dallas Seminary Press, 1947), IV, 256.

[2] Charles C. Ryrie, *The Bible and Tomorrow's News* (Wheaton: Scripture Press Publications, Inc., 1969), pp. 58,59.

[3] Rudolph Bultmann, *Kerygma and Myth* (London: S.P.C.K., 1954), p. 4

[4] Leslie H. Woodson, *Hell and Salvation* (Old Tappan, New Jersey: Fleming H. Revell Co., 1973), p. 24.

[5] *Ibid.*, p. 30.

CHAPTER 3

Divergent Evangelical Views of Major Unfulfilled Prophecies

Three major evangelical systems of thought offer explanations of God's plan and procedure for the future. Since they are evangelical, the adherents of each view is solidly Biblical and represents the true meaning of God's Word. Dedicated men and women who love the Lord and His Word hold to these views. Their honesty and sincerity must never be questioned. Yet, all three systems cannot fully represent the Biblical teaching because they are so different.

Each view has a different picture of what will take place when Christ returns to the earth. Will Christ return after the kingdom has already been realized? Will He establish an earthly kingdom and reign for 1000 years on David's throne in Jerusalem? Or will the eternal state be ushered in at His second coming?

Other sharp distinctions exist between the major interpretations of things to come, but basic to them all is the question, Will Christ institute the Davidic kingdom or will He usher in the eternal state when He comes again?

We want to present the three systems of thought along with important variations which are true of each. No defense will be given of any of the views. Our purpose here is simply to show the different views of unfulfilled prophecy as held by evangelicals.

Nonevangelicals or nonconservatives of all religious varieties usually have such a weak view of the Bible and its authority that they find no difficulty doing with prophecy what they do with most of the Bible—reject it and treat it as mythological and purely symbolic without any literal meaning at all. In short, they do not take Scripture seriously.

An example of the contemporary liberal view will show the contrast with the evangelical belief. C.H. Dodd in his *The Parables of the Kingdom* made famous the phrase "realized eschatology." In general, all non-evangelicals agree with Dodd on his view of unfulfilled prophecies.

According to his view, all eschatology—the doctrine of future things—was fulfilled at the incarnation of Christ. He arrives at his view by a process of wholesale discrediting of Scripture. With apparent ease he calls much of the Bible fraudulent. What is not fraudulent he either explains away or distorts to fit his presuppositions. He even goes so far as to say that Christ was simply mistaken in some of His prophecies. The Lord Jesus Christ was wrong!

But among those who do accept the divine authority of Holy Scripture and who do therefore take it seriously there are three major views about the future program of God for mankind and the world. The distinctions between these systems of belief are by no means imaginary or unimportant. To the contrary, there are far-reaching consequences associated with each of the views. These will now be presented as they developed in the history of the church.

PREMILLENNIALISM

Definition

The word *millennium* comes from the Latin words *mille* meaning thousand and *annus* meaning year. Though not found in the Bible, its Greek equivalent appears six times in Revelation 20. A designated period of time is meant by the word. Belief in such a period of time has been called chiliasm or millenarianism. The prefix *pre* before the word millennium refers to Christ's coming and thus premillennialism refers to the belief that Christ will return before the millennium and in fact will establish it when He returns to the earth.

Charles Ryrie, a distinguished defender of the premillennial system of thought, defined it this way: "In general the premillennial system may be characterized as follows: Premillennialists believe that theirs is the historic faith of the Church. Holding to a literal interpretation of the Scriptures, they believe that the promises made to Abraham and David are unconditional and have had or will have a literal fulfillment. In no sense have these promises made to Israel been abrogated or fulfilled by the Church, which is a distinct body in this age having promises and a destiny different from Israel's. At the close of this age, premillennialists believe that Christ will return for His Church, meeting her in the air (this is not the Second Coming of Christ), which event, called the rapture or translation, will usher in a seven-year period of tribulation on the earth. After this, the Lord will return to the earth (this is the Second Coming of Christ), to establish His kingdom on the earth for a thousand years, during which time the promises to Israel will be fulfilled."[1]

Differences

Premillennialists are all agreed that when Christ returns to the earth, He will institute the kingdom promised to David. Christ's second coming in power and great glory is not followed immediately by the eternal state. Instead, it is the one-thousand-year earthly rule of Christ which begins at that time. Old Testament promises to Israel are then fulfilled. The covenants God made with Abraham (Genesis 12) and David (II Samuel 7) and others are then realized.

Is there going to be in the future a seven-year period of unprecedented tribulation which will be the outpouring of God's wrath upon the world? Will this be what Jeremiah called the time of Jacob's trouble, a time of divine judgment unlike any other (Jeremiah 30:7)? Did Jesus refer to this time when He told His disciples there would "be great tribulation, such as was not since the beginning of the world to this time, no, nor ever shall be" (Matthew 24:21)?

Premillennialists would be in general agreement in answering "yes" to all the above questions.

Will the church, the body of Christ, be called upon to go through the future seven-year period of tribulation? Premillennialists give different answers to this question. They are not all agreed on the order in which some of the future events will transpire. For example, there are at least four different views of the relation of the church, which is Christ's body, to the coming tribulation.

• *The church to be raptured before the tribulation begins.* Some believe the entire church will be raptured, caught up to be with the Lord, before any part of the future seven-year tribulation begins. Those who hold this view are called pretribulationists.

John F. Walvoord, a widely recognized authority and spokesman for premillennial pretribulation defined the position this way: "The pretribulational interpretation

35

regards the coming of the Lord and the translation of the church as preceding immediately the fulfillment of Daniel's prophecy of a final seven-year period before the second advent. Based on a literal interpretation of Daniel's prophecy, it is held that there has been no fulfillment of Daniel 9:27 in history, and that therefore it prophesies a future period, familiarly called 'the tribulation.' The seven years of Daniel, bringing to a close the program of Israel prior to the second advent, will, therefore, be fullfilled between the translation of the church and the second advent of Christ to establish His kingdom on earth. At the translation, before the seven years, Christ will return to meet the church in the air; at the second advent, after the seven years, it is held that Christ will return with His Church from heaven to establish His millennial reign on earth."[2]

Pretribulationists find in Scripture a definite distinction between God's program with Israel and His program with the church. They also see a difference between Christ's coming *for* His own and His coming *with* His own. The coming *for* His own they call the "rapture." Christ's coming with His own to the earth is called the "second coming." At least one thousand years for the earthly reign of Christ and seven years of tribulation on the earth come between these two in this view.

Pretribulationalists are also dispensationalists. A dispensationalist is one who sees clear distinction in the Bible between God's program with the nation Israel and His program with the church. Dispensationalists believe the church began on the day of Pentecost as a distinct entity from Israel. According to dispensationalists God has dealt differently with His people at different times. They teach there has always been only one way of salvation—by grace through faith and altogether apart from human works. Even though they do not find their system clearly delineated in the early history of the church, they do insist its basic tenets were there.

Dr. Ryrie presents this concise definition of a dispensation: "A dispensation is a distinguishable economy in the outworking of God's purpose."[3] Describing the dispensational system of Biblical interpretation he said: "Dispensationalism views the world as a household run by God. In this household-world God is dispensing or administering its affairs according to His own will and in various stages of revelation in the process of time. These various stages mark off the distinguishably different economies in the outworking of His total purpose, and these economies are the dispensations. The understanding of God's differing economies is essential to a proper interpretation of His revelation within those various economies."[4]

Basic to the pretribulational view is belief in the imminent hope which is that Christ could come at any time. There are no unfulfilled prophecies awaiting fulfillment before His return in the air for His own. Among premillennial pretribulationists there is general agreement on the order of events in the future. A listing of these events will be helpful in understanding the view.

1. Increase in apostasy as this age draws to a close (I Timothy 4:1-3; II Timothy 3:1-5).

2. Resurrection of the dead in Christ, the translation of the living saints and the rapture of both groups (I Corinthians 15:20-24,35-50; I Thessalonians 4:13-18).

3. The seven-year tribulation on earth (Revelation 6—16). Those resurrected and translated are with the Lord in heaven. The Judgment Seat of Christ (I Corinthians 3:12-15) and the Marriage of the Lamb takes place (Revelation 19:7).

4. The Battle of Armageddon and the end of the tribulation. Christ comes with His own (Revelation 19:11-16). When Christ comes, Israel will be regathered and judged (Matthew 24:37—25:46). The Gentile nations will also be judged (Matthew 25:31-46).

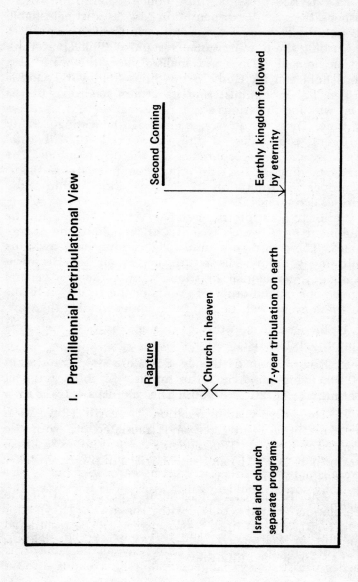

I. Premillennial Pretribulational View

Rapture

Second Coming

Church in heaven

7-year tribulation on earth

Earthly kingdom followed by eternity

Israel and church separate programs

38

5. The millennial reign of Christ begins. It will be 1000 years in length (Revelation 20:1-6). Before it begins, Satan is bound in the bottomless pit (Revelation 20:1). After the 1000 year reign Satan will be loosed for a little season (Revelation 20:7). He will deceive the people, lead a revolt against God, be defeated by Christ and then cast into the lake of fire (Revelation 20:10).

6. The Great White Throne Judgment (Revelation 20:11-15) occurs at which all the unsaved of all the ages appear and are cast into the lake of fire.

7. Creation of a new heaven and a new earth (Revelation 21:1).

8. Eternity (Revelation 22).

The *Premillennial Pretribulational View* diagram *(I.)* depicts the basic view now under discussion. By far, this is the most prominent view among premillennialists.

• *The church to go through the tribulation.* Some who insist they are premillennial have raised serious question with the belief that the church will escape the future seven-year tribulation. They do not believe the church will be raptured or caught up to meet the Lord in the air before the tribulation begins on earth. Rather, it is their contention that the church must pass through the period called in Scripture the time of Jacob's trouble. God will protect or preserve His own through this time, they insist. This view is called posttribulationalism and is common among amillennialists and postmillennialists, but is also held by some premillennialists. Alexander Reese gave this definition of premillennial posttribulation: "The Church of Christ will not be removed from the earth until the Advent of Christ at the very end of the present Age: the Rapture and the Appearing take place at the same crisis; hence Christians of that generation will be exposed to the final affliction under Antichrist."[5] The number of premillennialists who embrace posttribulationalism has been increasing lately and the position is gaining stature.

Considerable difference exists between evangelicals who are posttribulational. Those who do not subscribe to premillennialism believe the tribulation began with the early church.[6] Some even say it began with Adam.[7] But posttribulationalists who are premillennial take Scripture which speaks of great tribulation (Jeremiah 30:7; Daniel 12:1; Matthew 24:21) as unfulfilled but to be fulfilled in the future.[8]

In the premillennial posttribulational position little distinction is made between Christ's coming *for* His own in the rapture and His coming to the earth *with* His own to establish the kingdom. Distinction between God's program for Israel and His program for the church is even less distinct. The imminent hope is either denied or reinterpreted.

Posttribulationists are not dispensationalists,[9] and they do not present an order of future events. We may safely say, though, that they all believe the church will go through the coming tribulation. Christ's coming *for* His own and His coming *with* His own are seen as at the same time. There will be a resurrection and judgment of men and angels before the eternal state begins. The *Premillennial Posttribulational View* diagram *(II.)* pictures this position.

• *The church to go through the first half of the tribulation.* There are also some premillennialists who believe the church will pass through half of the future tribulation. The last half of the seventieth week of Daniel 9:24-27 is seen to be far more severe than the first half. This view has the church raptured in the middle of the week or in the middle of the tribulation and is known as the midtribulational view. It is a rather new explanation of the relation of the church to the coming tribulation. Midtribulationists do not usually use the term midtribula-

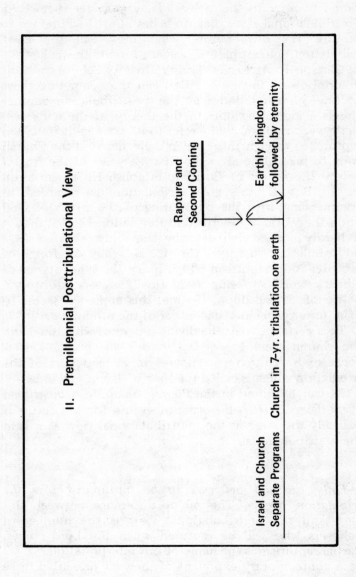

II. Premillennial Posttribulational View

Rapture and
Second Coming

Earthly kingdom
followed by eternity

Israel and Church
Separate Programs   Church in 7-yr. tribulation on earth

41

tional to refer to themselves. They consider themselves pretribulational since they do believe Christ will return to rapture His own before what they call the great tribulation, the last half of Daniel's seventieth week.[10]

Gleason L. Archer of Trinity Divinity School gave this description of the view: "Between the competing views of the pretribulation and the posttribulation rapture stands a mediating option, the theory of the midseventieth week rapture. Some refer to it as the midtribulation rapture, as though this sudden deliverance of the Church were to take place after the first 3½ years of the final 7 before the return of Christ to establish His kingdom on earth. But if the great tribulation is regarded as commencing with the outpouring of the wrath of God upon the world as described in Revelation 16—18, then it is hardly accurate to describe the midweek view as a midtribulation theory, for it is really a form of pretribulation rapturism which limits the time interval of climatic world suffering to the final 3½ years prior to the battle of Armageddon. To me, this approach seems to offer fewer problems than either of the other views."[11]

To a certain extent the divine programs with Israel and the church seem to overlap in this viewpoint. This is because the church participates in at least part of the tribulation which is called the time of Jacob's trouble.

As can be noted in the *Premillennial Midtribulational View* diagram *(III.)*, the order of events for the future is basically the same in the midtribulational view as it is in the pretribulational.

• *Only spiritual believers to be raptured before the tribulation begins.* The major difference between this view and the pretribulational view is the number of believers who will be raptured when the Lord comes. Partial rapturism is the name of this interpretation.

A contemporary exponent of the view presented three

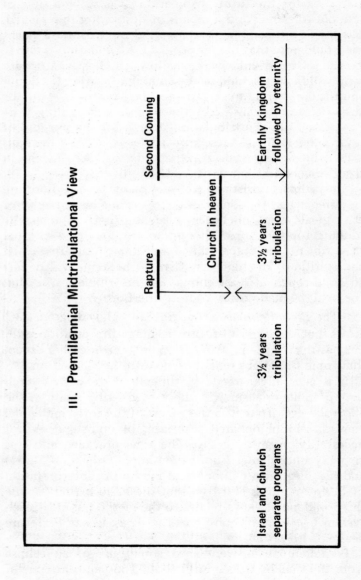

III. Premillennial Midtribulational View

Second Coming

Earthly kingdom
followed by eternity

Church in heaven

Rapture

3½ years
tribulation

3½ years
tribulation

Israel and church
separate programs

43

purposes for the future tribulation. It is to be a time of trouble for Israel and a means of destroying the wicked. His third purpose reveals his partial rapturism: "Finally, we would note that the purpose of the tribulation is also to be the testing of lukewarm, shallow, Laodicean Christians who will be left behind at the coming of Christ. No doubt multitudes who expected to be raptured will be disappointed because like the foolish virgins they were not watchful. The tribulation then is for the purpose of trying the faith of these who professed to be Christians but who really never repented or are living in disobedience to the will of God."[12]

Only those Christians who are ready for the Lord are raptured when He comes. And how is one made ready for that great event? Believers evidence their readiness by looking for the Lord. Those who are not living spiritual lives will not be prepared and will not be raptured when the spiritual Christians are. Carnal Christians will be left to go through at least enough of the tribulation so that they will be made ready to meet the Lord.

The *Premillennial Partial Rapture View* diagram *(IV.)* shows that the order of future events in this position is the same as that of the pretribulation order given earlier except that some Christians remain to go into the tribulation.

It is generally agreed by students of the early church that premillennialism was the view held by many in the apostolic age. That it is the oldest of the three millennial views is seldom debated. But age, of course, does not necessarily mean accuracy. The view prevailed and was virtually unchallenged until the time of Origen (185-254) and his allegorical or nonliteral method of interpretation of Scripture. It is still true that the basic reason for the three millennial views relates to the method used by each system in its interpretation of those passages of Scripture dealing with prophecy.

Premillennialism went into something of an eclipse from the time of Origen until about 1830 and the time of

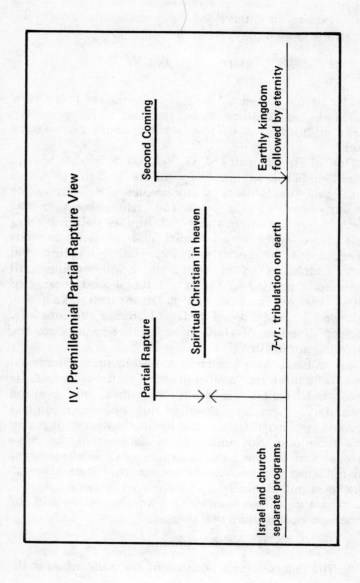

IV. Premillennial Partial Rapture View

Partial Rapture

Second Coming

Spiritual Christian in heaven

Israel and church
separate programs

7-yr. tribulation on earth

Earthly kingdom
followed by eternity

45

the prophetic Bible conferences. It was revived at that time. During the intervening years amillennialism was the prevailing system of belief.

AMILLENNIALISM

Definition
The prefix *a* means "no." Amillennialism is the view which denies a future literal reign of Christ upon the earth in fulfillment of the Old Testament promises of God.

One of its advocates, J. G. Vos has defined it thusly: "Amillennialism is that view of the last things which holds that the Bible does not predict a 'millennium' or period of world wide peace and righteousness on this earth before the end of the world. Amillennialism teaches that there will be a parallel and contemporaneous development of good and evil—God's kingdom and Satan's kingdom—in this world, which will continue until the second coming of Christ. At the second coming of Christ the resurrection and judgment will take place, followed by the eternal order of things—the absolute, perfect Kingdom of God, in which there will be no sin, suffering nor death."[13]

Jay Adams, who embraces the amillennial interpretation, calls the term "amillennialism" an unhappy one. He does not believe it really describes the position accurately. "*Amillennialism* is not only a misnomer because it is negative, but the distinction which it makes is a false one. No amillennialist denies that the Bible teaches a millennium. But the word *amillennialism* means no millennium. The issue is not whether Revelation 20 teaches a millennium. All amillennialists believe it does . . . . The true difference between amillennialism and the other systems involves two things:

1. The nature of the millennium.

2. The chronological position of the millennium in the

economy of God.

The word *amillennialism* fails to draw either of these distinctions. Instead, it expresses a belief which no conservative holds—that there is no millennium. The term cannot be defended, and certainly should be abandoned. Amillennialists simply are not amillennialists!"[14]

A new term is suggested by Adams to refer to the position which he embraces and which has been known as amillennialism. "Accurately speaking, the biblical system may be distinguished from the two other systems as *realized millennialism.* Whereas both pre- and postmillennialists look forward to a future unrealized millennium, realized millennialists contend that the millennium is a present reality. This chronological difference necessarily involves the *nature* of the period. If the millennium is a present reality, it is most certainly of a non-utopian type. Both of the other systems maintain that the millennium is future exactly *because* they cannot conceive of its nature as identical with the present church age. Both wrongly look for an earthly utopia apart from that fiery purging which alone will bring what the Bible calls 'the new earth.' They anticipate a golden age prior to the judgment of all men. Adherents to *realized* millennialism, on the other hand, maintain that such a belief confounds the millennium with the eternal state described in the last two chapters of Revelation, II Peter 3:12-14, Isaiah 65:17, and other prophecies. While realized millennialists believe there is a future golden age, they teach that it follows the millennial period. It will not come until the old earth has 'fled away' (Rev. 20:11)."[15]

Maybe the term *realized millennialism* is a better description of the positions traditionally known as amillennialism. The fact still remains, regardless of what the view is called, this interpretation does not allow for a future earthly kingdom. To that extent it is distinct from premillennialism and postmillenialism.

Amillennialists all reject dispensationalism. They believe it is a rather recent human invention foisted upon the Scriptures. In place of dispensational theology amillennialists and postmillennialists, for that matter, substitute what is known as convenant theology. "It represents the whole of Scripture as being covered by two covenants: (1) the covenant of works, and (2) the covenant of grace."[16]

The covenant of works was an agreement between God and Adam. God promised him life for obedience and death for disobedience. Adam and mankind in him failed of course. To save man from the penalty of his disobedience the covenant of grace became operative. It is the agreement between the offended God and the offending but elect sinner in which God promises salvation through Christ. A covenant of redemption is also usually included in the system. This covenant was the agreement in eternity past between the Father, Son, and Holy Spirit as to each one's part in the redemptive plan of God.

The covenants in covenant theology—redemption, works, grace—must not be confused with covenants such as the Abrahamic and Davidic. In convenant theology these Biblical covenants are made to be subservient to the covenant of grace. Dispensationalism, on the contrary, places primary emphasis upon the clearly stated Biblical covenants without denying the covenants in convenant theology. In other words, covenant theology and dispensationalism are very different. The former understands the Bible on the basis of the covenant of grace and the latter understands it more on the basis of the Abrahamic, Davidic, Palestinian and new covenants.

Differences

Amillennialists are also divided. In their case division comes over the exact way to interpret Scripture which

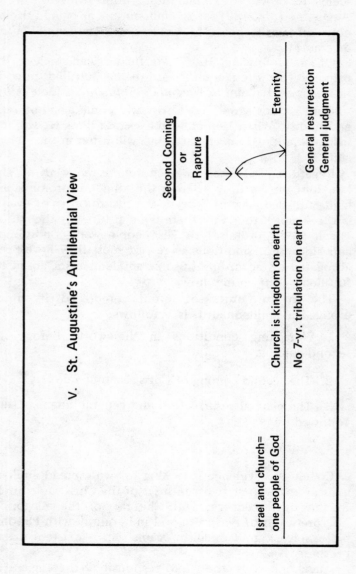

V. St. Augustine's Amillennial View

Israel and church=
one people of God

Church is kingdom on earth

No 7-yr. tribulation on earth

Second Coming
or
Rapture

Eternity

General resurrection
General judgment

seems to describe a millennium. Some who follow St. Augustine (354-430) see the millennium as being fulfilled now on earth. See *St. Augustine's Amillennial View* diagram *(V.)*.

Others following B. B. Warfield's lead believe the promises of a millennium are being fulfilled now in heaven. See diagram of *Warfield's Amillennial View (VI.)*.

Both groups agree that Christ will come again literally and bodily. When He comes the second time, He will not institute a kingdom on earth but will usher in the eternal state.

Regardless whether the church is viewed as the kingdom on earth or whether the kingdom promises are being fulfilled now in heaven, the future order of events is the same. Either way there is no future for the nation Israel. God's promises to His people were conditional, and since the conditions were not met, they have been abrogated or, according to some amillennialists, are being fulfilled by the church now.

The future order of events embraced by most evangelical amillennialists is as follows:

1. Worsening conditions in the world before the second coming,

2. The second coming of Christ accompanied by

3. The general resurrection and general judgment, and followed by

4. Eternity.

Conclusive evidence is lacking for widespread amillennialism in the first two centuries of the Christian church. In the third century, with the rise of the allegorical interpretation of Scripture and in harmony with Platonic philosophy, amillennialism came into existence and prospered.

Augustine was the first responsible theologian to

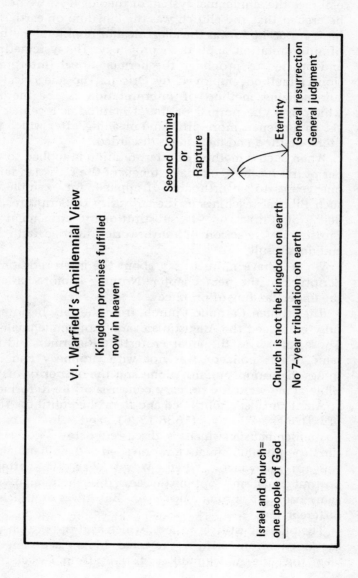

VI. Warfield's Amillennial View

Kingdom promises fulfilled
now in heaven

Second Coming
or
Rapture

Eternity

General resurrection
General judgment

Israel and church=
one people of God

Church is not the kingdom on earth

No 7-year tribulation on earth

embrace the amillennial system of theology. As we noted, he argued that the church was the kingdom on earth. His basis for doing so was the allegorical or nonliteral method of interpretation applied to prophecy. He systematized and applied to prophecy the hermeneutical (interpretational) method employed by Origen. The allegorical or spiritualizing method of interpretation is the method which uses the normal or literal method as a vehicle to get to a deeper, more profound meaning, after which the literal method and meaning is discarded.

When such a method of interpretation is applied to the Scriptural teaching on major tenets of the Christian faith, one ceases to be orthodox. If applied, for example, to such Biblical teachings as the authority of Scripture, the deity of Christ or the substitutionary atonement of Christ, only rejection of the historic Christian faith can and does result.

We will have more to say about the interpretation of Scripture in the next chapter. Nothing is more basic to the understanding of prophecy.

The Roman Catholic Church, from the very beginning, fully embraced the Augustinian variety of amillennialism. Those known as the great Protestant Reformers did the same. Their concern was not with prophecy and last things. Salvation by faith alone and the authority of the Bible alone were the primary concerns of the Reformers.

Amillennialism continued and flourished until the time of Daniel Whitby (1638-1726) and the rise of postmillennialism which is discussed below. For some time the postmillennial view prevailed and amillennialism was in abeyance. When World War II shattered postmillennialism's optimistic view, the amillennial view came back into prominence again. But it was of a slightly different sort.

The old Augustinian variety, which said the church was the kingdom on earth, was rejected. In its place came the view that the millennium is distinct from the church.

Christ's kingdom was said to be heavenly, not earthly. The kingdom promises in the Bible were fulfilled in the state of blessedness of the saints in heaven and in Christ's position at the right hand of the Father. In other words, Christ's present session was the fulfillment of the kingdom promises in the Old Testament. This is the variety of amillennialism commonly held by evangelicals today.

POSTMILLENNIALISM

Definition

According to this system, as held by evangelicals, Christ will return after society has been Christianized by the church. In this view the church is not the kingdom but it will, through the spread of the gospel, build it. *Post* prefixed before the word "millennium" means Christ will come after a kingdom has been established. The "thousand years" of Revelation 20 or the millennium are not taken literally.

The Baptist theologian, Augustus Hopkins Strong, who subscribed to postmillennialism, described the view this way: "The Scripture foretells a period, called in the language of prophecy 'a thousand years,' when Satan shall be restrained and the saints shall reign with Christ on the earth. A comparison of the passages bearing on this subject leads us to the conclusion that this millennial blessedness and dominion is prior to the Second Advent."[17]

Loraine Boettner, a contemporary postmillennial theologian, defines the system in these words: "Postmillennialism is that view of the last things which holds that the Kingdom of God is now being extended in the world through the preaching of the Gospel and the saving work of the Holy Spirit, that the world eventually will be Christianized, and that the return of Christ will occur at the close of a long period of righteousness and peace commonly called the *Millennium* . . . It should be added that on postmillennial principles the second coming of Christ will be followed immediately by the general resurrection, the general judgment, and the introduction of heaven and hell in their fulness."[18]

Actually, evangelical postmillennialism differs from evangelical amillennialism primarily in its belief in the final triumph of good over evil before Christ returns. Some postmillennialists believe the entire church or interadvent age is the millennium. Others believe the Christianizing of society will come gradually and be fully realized at a time in the remote future but before the return of Christ. For the postmillennialist, Christ's coming closes this age and is followed by the eternal state. And that is also believed by amillennialists.

Rise and Development

Until rather recently postmillennialism was a most important and influential millennial view. It arose in the mid-seventeenth century as a result of and a reaction against humanism and liberal theology.

The near demise of postmillennialism came with the collapse of utopian dreams in the World Wars. Today it is a minority view among evangelicals. Also, postmillennialism found it almost impossible to stem the tide toward liberal theology. The nonliteral method of prophetic interpretation, on which both postmillennialism and amillennialism rests, does leave the door open wide for the same kind of interpretation to be applied to other Biblical matters. With both systems the perplexing question remains, If certain prophecies can be spiritualized, why cannot other prophecies and teachings of the Bible also be spiritualized?

Differences

Evangelical postmillennialism, defined above, must of course be distinguished from the now rather outdated theologically liberal view which teaches that a kingdom

54

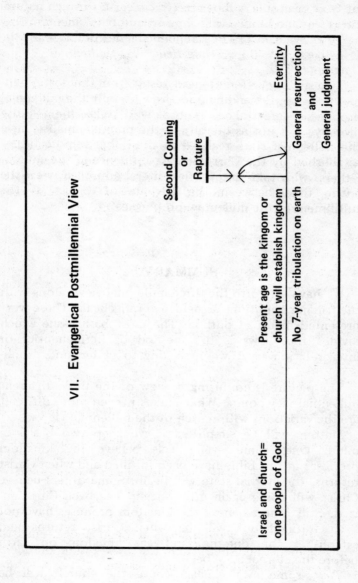

VII. Evangelical Postmillennial View

Israel and church= one people of God

Present age is the kingom or church will establish kingdom

No 7-year tribulation on earth

Second Coming or Rapture

Eternity

General resurrection and General judgment

of God or utopia will be created on earth through natural processes and human achievement and betterment.

The evangelical postmillennial viewpoint may be visualized in the *Evangelical Postmillennial View* diagram *(VII.)*.

Two slightly different views result from the postmillennial position, depending upon how literally the millennial prophecies are taken. Those who take them quite literally, yet not as literally as the premillennialist, have the millennial state realized in the rather remote future established by the Christianizing influence of the church. Others, who take an even less literal approach, view the entire time between the advents of Christ as the fulfillment of the millennial prophecies.

SUMMARY

We have set forth the three millennial views along with their major variations as held by evangelicals. These were presented in broad outline. The most basic issue which divides the views is the method of hermeneutics or interpretation used when seeking to understand prophecy.

The picture is confusing in view of the three different millennial viewpoints. What makes it even more difficult are the variations within each of the millennial views.

Matters will be simplified if we keep two basics in mind. *One,* some evangelicals believe the kingdom promises in the Bible have been fulfilled and when Christ returns, the eternal state will begin. Some others believe Christ will come again after society has been Christianized. Still others believe the kingdom promises have not been fulfilled but will be when Christ returns and establishes the one-thousand-year kingdom on earth before the eternal state begins.

Two, some evangelicals believe the church will be

protected but will go through the future seven-year period of tribulation. Others believe the entire church will be raptured before any part of the tribulation begins, while some believe that only spiritual believers will be raptured before the tribulation begins. Still others hold that the church will experience part of the tribulation.

These are the broad differences among evangelicals over things to come. In our next chapter we want to address the question, Why do these differences over unfulfilled prophecy exist among evangelicals?

NOTES FOR CHAPTER 3

[1] Charles C. Ryrie, *The Basis of the Premillennial Faith* (New York: Loizeaux Brothers, 1953), p. 12.

[2] John F. Walvoord, *The Rapture Question* (Findlay, Ohio: Dunham Publishing Company, 1957), p. 51.

[3] Ryrie, *Dispensationalism Today* (Chicago: Moody Press, 1965), p. 29.

[4] *Ibid.*, p. 31.

[5] Alexander Reese, *The Approaching Advent of Christ* (London: Marshall, Morgan & Scott, Limited, [n.d.]), p. 18.

[6] George L. Rose, *Tribulation Till Translation* (Glendale, Calif.: Rose Publishing Co., 1943), pp. 68,69.

[7] George H. Fromow, *Will the Church Pass Through the Great Tribulation?* (London: The Sovereign Grace Advent Testimony, [n.d.]).

[8] George E. Ladd, *The Blessed Hope* (Grand Rapids: Eerdmans, 1956), pp. 72-77 and Robert H. Gundry, *The Church and the Tribulation* (Grand Rapids: Zondervan, 1973).

[9] A recent exception to this is Robert H. Gundry in his *The Church and the Tribulation,* pp. 12-28.

[10] Norman B. Harrison, *The End* (Minneapolis: The Harrison Service, 1941), p. 118.

[11] Gleason L. Archer, "Jesus Is Coming Again: Midtribulation," *Christian Life* (May, 1974), p. 21.

[12] Ray Brubaker, "The Purpose of the Tribulation," *Radar News* (Dec., 1968), p. 6.

[13] J. G. Vox, *Blue Banner Faith and Life* (January-March, 1951) cited from Loraine Boettner, *The Millennium* (Philadelphia: The Presbyterian and Reformed Publishing Co., 1964), p. 109.

[14] Jay Adams, *The Time Is at Hand* (Nutley, New Jersey: The Presbyterian and Reformed Publishing Co., 1966), p. 8.

[15] *Ibid*, p. 9.

[16] George N. M. Collins, "Covenant Theology," *Baker's Dictionary of Theology* (Grand Rapids: Baker Book House, 1960), p. 144.

[17] Augustus Hopkins Strong, *Systematic Theology* (Philadelphia: American Baptist Publication Society, 1907), III, 1010-11.

[18] Loraine Boettner, *The Millennium,* pp. 4,14.

CHAPTER 4

Why
the Different Views
of Things to Come?

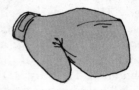

Evangelicals who defend a particular view of things to come do not all understand Scripture in the same way. That, of course, is obvious, as we have just seen. The reason they understand it differently is because they do not all use the same method of interpreting the unfulfilled prophecy of Scripture. This is the most basic reason for the differences over *pre*, *a* or *post* millennialism. It also has much to do with the differences over the relation of the church to the coming great tribulation.

The science and art of Biblical interpretation is called "hermeneutics." And it is easy to see that a method of interpretation, a system of hermeneutics, is most important to the understanding of God's Word.[1]

Without it the Bible is really a closed book. And of course that is true of all literature. Whenever we read anything, we often unconsciously follow certain rules of interpretation so we can understand the material. "What does this mean?" is the question every reader asks.

The interpretation of Scripture is one of several crucial matters related to the total doctrine of Scripture. A brief review of these related matters will help us put things in focus before we discuss the bearing interpretation has upon the differences over things to come.

PUTTING THINGS IN FOCUS

The meaning or interpretation of Scripture is related to revelation, inspiration, authority, canonicity, and illumination.

Revelation, in reference to Scripture, means the act of God whereby He made Himself and His will known to man. God gave the revelation; man received it.

Inspiration has to do with the recording of the revelation. When we speak of the inspiration of the Bible, like Paul did in II Timothy 3:16-17, we are referring to God's work of guiding and controlling the human writers of Scripture in the very choice of the words they wrote in the original autographs. The result of this divine work upon the fallible human penman was the recording of God's message to man without error or omission in all its parts.

Because the revelation recorded without error in the Bible came from God, it is of course divinely authoritative. It bears the very *authority* of the One who gave it.

The God who gave His Word also preserved it for us. From the very time the revelation was given and recorded, it was accepted by God's people as His Word. The human recognition of God's Word by His people we call the *canonization* of Scripture.

The Holy Spirit who was used in the giving, receiving,

and acknowledging of God's Word also enables the child of God to understand it. This we call *illumination*.

My purpose in presenting this brief background in the doctrine of Scripture has been to distinguish the science of Biblical interpretation from the other facets of the doctrine and to show its relation to them.

I want to make clear too that evangelicals agree and have little difference when it comes to revelation, inspiration, authority, canonicity, and illumination of Scripture. But they do not agree on a method of interpretation to be followed uniformly throughout the Bible.

Is there a single method of interpretation to be used in all the Bible? Or, does some Scripture require a different method? It is over this issue that evangelicals are greatly divided. And as a result of the great division, prophecy is in the ring.

IMPORTANCE OF THE ISSUE

When it comes to the understanding of prophecy of things to come, the first and most important question is, How is it to be interpreted? What does this prophetic Scripture mean? That is the all-important question. And it is admitted candidly by representative spokesmen of each of the various evangelical views of things to come that this is the case. All must agree, though some are more reluctant to admit it than others, that they differ over things to come because they interpret the prophecies differently.

Observe a few admissions which illustrate my point.

Oswald T. Allis put the issue bluntly. His book *Prophecy and the Church* was intended to show the error in premillennial dispensationalism and to defend his own view of amillennialism. He said, ". . . Old Testament prophecies if literally interpreted cannot be regarded as having been yet fulfilled or as being capable of fulfillment in this present age. It is consequently assumed by premillennialists that they will be so fulfilled during the millennium when Satan will be bound and the saints will reign with Christ."[2]

A more contemporary amillennial writer reflected the same view in these words: "One very basic conflict between different millennial groups is their hermeneutics —the manner in which they interpret the Bible. In fact, this difference is what divides equally conservative men into differing camps with reference to the millennium. This fact is acknowledged frequently by all millennial schools of thought. Each of the millennial views has been held by conservative, scholarly men who were devoted to a correct interpretation of the Bible and all have looked on the Scriptures as divinely inspired, and as the Christian's only rule of faith and life."[3]

In his recent book, *The Time Is at Hand*, Jay Adams also revealed the importance of the interpretation of unfulfilled prophecy: "In this transition from pre to posttribulationism, some have gone further, and are beginning to test the foundations of premillennialism itself. In the process, doubts about fundamental presuppositions have arisen. Having rejected the un-biblical principle of exclusively literal interpretation of Old Testament prophecy, many no longer look upon so-called 'national Israel' as God's chosen people. They cannot agree to a 'Jewish' millennium, fully equipped with rebuilt temple and restored sacrificial system. They find no indication of a utopian-type millennium anywhere upon the pages of the New Testament."[4]

Loraine Boettner, evangelical postmillennial theologian, expressed his awareness of the crucial importance of one's method of interpretation. He agrees the basic reason for different views of things to come has to do with principles of Biblical interpretation. "That believing Christians through the ages, using the same Bible and acknowledging it to be authoritative, have arrived at quite different conclusions appears to be due primarily to different methods of interpretation. Premillennialists place strong emphasis on literal interpretation and pride themselves on taking Scripture just as it is written. Post- and Amillennialists on the other hand, mindful of the fact that much of both the Old and New Testament unquestionably is given in figurative or symbolic language, have no objection on principle against figurative interpretation and readily accept that if the evidence indicates that it is preferable."[5]

But amillennialists and postmillennialists are not alone in acknowledging the importance of Biblical interpretation for an understanding of things to come. Premillennialists also agree wholeheartedly. Their writings on the future are filled with emphatic statements on this point.

The Theocratic Kingdom of Our Lord Jesus, the Christ is a classic three-volume set in defense of premillennialism. In it George N. H. Peters states his view of the importance of a proper method of interpretation: "The literal, grammatical interpretation of the Scriptures must (connected with the figurative, tropical [sic], or rhetorical) be observed in order to obtain a correct understanding of this kingdom . . . Its import is of such weight; the consequences of its adoption are of such moment; the tendency it possesses of leading to the truth and of vindicating Scripture is of such value, that we cannot pass it by without some explanations and reflections."[6]

A contemporary spokesman for premillennialism voiced the same understanding of the importance of the interpretation of prophecy: "There is a growing realization in the theological world that the crux of the millennial issue is the question of *method* of interpreting Scripture. Premillenarians follow the so-called 'grammatical-historical' literal interpretation while amillenarians use a spiritualizing method."[7]

It is an accepted fact. Nobody debates the issue. The

method of interpretation one uses is critical to his understanding of what he reads. This is no less true of the prophetic Scripture than of any other literature.

What methods of interpretation are available? Which ones are used by the differing schools of thought with respect to the future? These questions must now be answered.

THE METHODS OF INTERPRETATION

Two methods of interpreting the Bible are prominent today. Other methods have been suggested in the history of the church[8] but the literal or normal and the spiritualizing or allegorical methods have been and still are the most prominent and important methods.

The literal or normal method

Premillennial Christians usually pride themselves in their belief in the literal interpretation of all of Scripture. They are described frequently by friends and foes as literalists. They are sometimes called "wooden literalists" which charge implies they do not allow for types and symbols in their understanding of Scripture. But that criticism doesn't seem to square with the fact that premillennial writers have contributed most to the understanding of these.

By a literal interpretation of Scripture premillennialists mean a normal interpretation. To them the Bible is to be interpreted just like all other literature. "The literal interpretation as applied to any document is that view which adopts as the sense of a sentence the meaning of that sentence in usual, or ordinary, or normal conversation or writing."[9] "To interpret literally means nothing more or less than to interpret in terms of normal, usual, designation."[10]

Premillennialists are agreed in accepting the above as an accurate definition and description of their method of interpreting the whole Bible.

The literal or normal method of interpreting Scripture is also called the grammatical-historical method. This designation emphasizes that the meaning of Scripture in the method is determined both by the grammatical and the historical considerations.

Premillennial dispensationalists have not failed to support their use of the literal, normal, or plain interpretation of Scripture. Many reasons are given by them in defense of their position.[11]

All of their defense seems really to revolve around and relate to three crucial reasons: "Philosophically, the purpose of language itself seems to require literal interpretation. Language was given by God for the purpose of being able to communicate with man . . . If God be the originator of language and if the chief purpose of originating it was to convey His message to man, then it must follow that He, being all-wise and all-loving, originated sufficient language to convey all that was in His heart to tell man . . . A second reason why dispensationalists believe in the literal principle is a Biblical one. It is simply this: the prophecies in the Old Testament concerning the first coming of Christ—His birth, His rearing, His ministry, His death, His resurrection—were all fulfilled literally. There is no non-literal fulfillment of these prophecies in the New Testament . . . A third reason is a logical one. If one does not use the plain, normal, or literal method of interpretation, all objectivity is lost. What check would there be on the variety of interpretations which man's imagination could produce if there were not an objective standard which the literal principle provides?"[12]

Premillennialists insist that the New Testament's use of the Old Testament substantiates the literal method. In support of this, reference is often made, as in the above, to the many Old Testament prophecies which were literally fulfilled in the New Testament. Why, premillennialists agree, should we expect unfulfilled prophecies to be fulfilled in a different way from those already fulfilled?

Appeal is also made to Jesus' method of interpretation of the Old Testament. It is clear from His example that He used the normal, literal, plain method. Always, His interpretation of Scripture was in harmony with the grammatical and historical meaning. Frequently, Jesus interpreted one passage of Scripture by appealing to another passage to add further clarification to the meaning (i.e., Matthew 19:3-8 and Deuteronomy 24:1; cf. Matthew 12:3-7 and Hosea 6:6).

The spiritualizing or allegorizing method

According to proponents of the view it is simply impossible to apply the literal method of interpretation to all of Scripture. Amillennialists and postmillennialists insist on this.

Oswald T. Allis, for example, believe a thoroughly literal interpretation of Scripture is impossible.[13] He gives three major reasons for his belief. They are: "(1) The language of the Bible often contains figure of speech. This is especially true of its poetry . . . (2) The great theme of the Bible is, God and His redemptive dealings with mankind. God is a Spirit; the most precious teachings of the Bible are *spiritual;* and these spiritual and heavenly realities are often set forth under the form of earthly objects and human relationships . . . We should remember the saying of the apostle, that spiritual things are 'spiritually discerned' . . . (3) The fact that the Old Testament is both preliminary and preparatory to the New Testament is too obvious to require proof." [14] Premillennialists have often responded to these objections.[15]

It must be admitted that not until the third century A.D. and the Alexandrian school of theology was there any serious opposition to the literal method. Teachers in this school—Clement of Alexandria and Origen—used a method of interpretation which made all Scripture an allegory. In the fifth century Augustine led a rejection of such extremes. He insisted not upon a complete rejection of the allegorical method but that only prophecy needs to be allegorized or spiritualized. Much of Biblical truth was salvaged by Augustine's efforts. Yet he and many of his followers, including the great Reformers, continued to use the allegorical method in their interpretation of some unfulfilled prophecy.

Luther, Calvin, and others of the Reformers did stress the need for the literal sense of Scripture and for a grammatical historical approach. But they did not apply those principles to their interpretation of all unfulfilled prophecy.

Too, it must be admitted that the spiritualizing or allegorizing method of Biblical interpretation did not arise out of a desire to understand Scripture. It did not spring from pious desires. Instead, it owes its birth to heathen philosophy. "The allegorical system that arose among the pagan Greeks, copied by the Alexandrian Jews, was next adopted by the Christian church, and dominated the church to the Reformation."[16]

The allegorical or spiritualizing method of interpretation may be defined as "the method of interpreting a literary text that regards the literal sense as the vehicle for a secondary, more spiritual and more profound sense."[17]

Premillennialists believe such a method for seeking to understand the meaning of any part of Scripture has very serious dangers. They ask some very searching questions of such a method. What is the basic authority in interpretation—the Scriptures or the mind of the interpreter? They do not feel that the allegorical method really involves the interpretation of Scripture. It only can result in fanciful speculation. Too, how can the conclusions of the interpreter who uses this method be tested?

Don't all evangelical expositors of the Bible use the literal, historical-grammatical method? Could anybody possibly be evangelical if he didn't apply this method to the Biblical teaching about Christ, salvation, sin, etc? To be sure, when the allegorical method is employed with the passages presenting the cardinal doctrines of the faith, evangelicalism does not result. Only by following the literal, normal method does one come to embrace the essentials of the faith and avoid theological liberalism.

Premillennialists are convinced that the system of hermeneutics they use is a tremendous safeguard against liberal theology. And there does seem to be some validity to that claim.

True, all evangelicals do use the literal method for their understanding of most of the Bible. But it is also true that some, namely, those of amillennial and post-millennial persuasion, wish to use a less than literal hermeneutic with much unfulfilled prophecy. It is right at this point that the evangelical world is divided over things to come. This is what puts prophecy in the ring. Premillennialists can't understand why their Christian brothers insist on using a different method of interpretation with some unfulfilled prophecy but not with all of it. They believe strongly if some teachings may be understood in a less than literal way, the door is open for a nonliteral approach to any part of Scripture. "Why not?" they ask. On what grounds is the less than literal approach to be restricted to only some themes of unfulfilled prophecy?

To summarize the difference between the two schools of thought this may be said: All evangelicals use the literal method in their interpretation of the Bible. Some evangelicals believe this same method is to be used with all Scripture. These are the premillennialists. Other evangelicals believe that while the literal method is to be used with Scripture in general, it is not to be used with all unfulfilled prophetic portions. Some of the Biblical prophecies (i.e., those concerning the first advent of Christ) are to be understood literally and in fact were fulfilled literally.[18] Yet many prophecies related to the future coming again of Christ must be understood in a less than literal way. These are amillennial and postmillennial evangelicals.

THE METHODS AND THE COVENANTS

God made some staggering promises to His people through chosen representatives. These promises are presented to us in Scripture in the form of covenants. Evangelical Christians all agree with this. As you might suspect, what they do not all agree on is the nature and meaning of these covenants. To whom, specifically, were they given? Are they conditional, depending on man's obedience for their fulfillment, or are they unconditional, depending solely upon the "I will" of God for their fulfillment?

There are four basic covenants in the Old Testament which relate especially to things to come. In truth, it is not too much to say that one's view of these covenants determines his view of things to come. In each of these covenants God promised specific things to His own people.

Four Biblical Covenants

The *Four Biblical Covenants* diagram *(VIII.)* shows the importance of the Abrahamic covenant and the relation of the other three to it. The major features of the Abrahamic Covenant—land, seed, blessings—are each developed further in the later covenants.

What, in fact, did God promise in these Biblical covenants? Let us examine each of them to see what they include without respect to a particular view of things to come. Before we do that, we should seek to define a Biblical covenant. Frequently, the word *covenant* appears in the Bible. Relationships and agreements between God

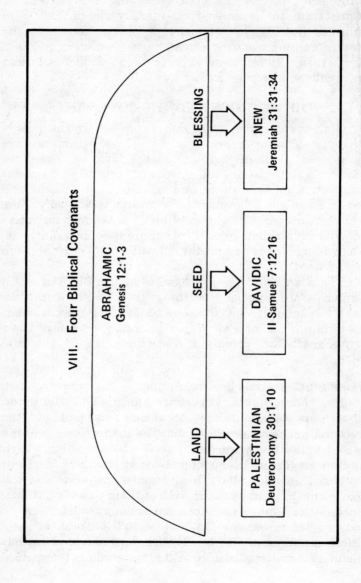

VIII. Four Biblical Covenants

ABRAHAMIC
Genesis 12:1-3

LAND

SEED

BLESSING

PALESTINIAN
Deuteronomy 30:1-10

DAVIDIC
II Samuel 7:12-16

NEW
Jeremiah 31:31-34

70

and man, between men, and even between nations are called covenants. As used in the Bible, a covenant is a compact, an agreement, a contract. Some of the covenants in Scripture are obviously conditional—the stated conditions must be met by both parties involved. Other Biblical covenants do not stress conditions and seem to be unconditional in nature; they depend solely for their fulfillment upon the truthfulness of the one who proposes and makes the covenant. In the case of the covenants we want to study now that One is God Himself.

The Abrahamic Covenant

"Now the Lord had said unto Abram, Get thee out of thy country, and from thy kindred, and from thy father's house, unto a land that I will shew thee: And I will make of thee a great nation, and I will bless thee, and make thy name great; and thou shalt be a blessing: And I will bless them that bless thee, and curse him that curseth thee: and in thee shall all families of the earth be blessed" (Genesis 12:1-3).

Confirmation and enlargement of this great covenant is recorded in several other Scriptures (i.e., Genesis 12:6,7; 13:14-17; 15:1-21; 17:1-14; 22:15-18; Psalms 69).

Just a normal reading of the passage reveals that some of the promises of God to Abraham were *personal*, some were concerned with the *nation* which would come from his loins, and others were *universal* in nature. It is generally not even debated that this is the case.

God promised to bless Abraham, give him a great name, make him a channel of blessing to others, deal with others as they dealt with him and his seed, and also to give him an heir by Sarah (Genesis 12:1-3; 15:4). These promises all concerned Abraham as an individual.

A great nation was to be born from Abraham's seed (Genesis 12:2 cf. 17:6). This nation was promised the land of Canaan as an everlasting inheritance (cf. Genesis

17:8). Also, God promised that the covenant would be established with Abraham's seed and it would be "everlasting" (Genesis 17:7).

God said to Abraham, "In thee shall all families of the earth be blessed" (Genesis 12:3). "All families of the earth" reached beyond Abraham and even beyond his physical seed. This aspect of the covenant is generally referred to as universal.

The burning question is, Have any of these promises to Abraham, the father of the Jewish race, been fulfilled? Has fulfillment of all of them occurred? If any of them have been fulfilled, which ones are they? How were they fulfilled? What about the remaining promises? Does the nation Israel really have a future in God's program? The answers to these and other similar questions have great bearing upon one's view of things to come. As soon as we ask questions like these, we are stepping inside the ring, where the action is.

The Palestinian Covenant

The covenant is called Palestinian because it concerns the land of Palestine. At the close of Moses' leadership and when Joshua was about to begin his work, the people of Israel were still not in possession of the land God had promised them. They were at the entrance of it but not in it. In fact, there were enemies in the land. Was the land of Palestine really going to be theirs? Was God going to fulfill His promises in spite of all their own unbelief and in spite of the enemies' opposition?

God's answer to these questions came in the form of a covenant: "And it shall come to pass, when all these things are come upon thee, the blessing and the curse, which I have set before thee, and thou shalt call them to mind among all the nations, whither the Lord thy God hath driven thee, And shalt return unto the Lord thy God, and shalt obey his voice according to all that I command thee this day, thou and thy children, with all thine heart, and with all thy soul; That then the Lord thy God will turn thy captivity, and have compassion upon thee, and will return and gather thee from all the nations where the Lord thy God hath scattered thee. If any of thine be driven out unto the outmost parts of heaven, from there will the Lord thy God gather thee, and from there will he fetch thee. And the Lord thy God will bring thee into the land which thy fathers possessed, and thou shalt possess it; and he will do thee good, and multiply thee above thy fathers. And the Lord thy God will circumcise thine heart, and the heart of thy seed, to love the Lord thy God with all thine heart, and with all thy soul, that thou mayest live. And the Lord thy God will put all these curses upon thine enemies, and on them who hate thee, who persecuted thee. And thou shalt return and obey the voice of the Lord, and do all his commandments which I command thee this day. And the Lord thy God will make thee plenteous in every work of thine hand, in the fruit of thy body, and in the fruit of thy cattle, and in the fruit of thy land, for good; for the Lord will again rejoice over thee for good, as he rejoiced over thy fathers, If thou shalt hearken unto the voice of the Lord thy God, to keep his commandments and his statutes which are written in this book of the law, and if thou turn unto the Lord thy God with all thine heart, and with all thy soul" (Deuteronomy 30:1-10).

Notice several tremendous promises enumerated in this covenant. Because of unfaithfulness the nation would be taken from the land (verses 1-3 cf. Deuteronomy 28:63-68). Israel's Messiah would return (verse 3-6). Israel would be restored to the land (verse 5). As a nation, Israel would be judged (verse 7). Full blessing from God would come to the nation Israel in God's time (verse 9).

At a later time in Israel's history this covenant was confirmed by God Himself (Ezekiel 16:1-7). Apparently, it had not yet been all fulfilled by the time of Ezekiel's writing. Has the covenant ever been fulfilled completely? Has the nation Israel ever possessed all the land promised her by God in this covenant? Christians differ in their answers to such pertinent questions. Why do Christians "fight" about things to come? One reason is because they understand the Biblical covenants differently.

The Davidic Covenant

To David, God said: "And when thy days be fulfilled, and thou shalt sleep with thy fathers, I will set up thy seed after thee, which shall proceed out of thine own body, and I will establish his kingdom. He shall build an house for my name, and I will establish the throne of his kingdom forever. I will be his father, and he shall be my son. If he commit iniquity, I will chasten him with the rod of men, and with the stripes of the children of men; But my mercy shall not depart away from him, as I took it from Saul, whom I put away before thee. And thine house and thy kingdom shall be established forever before thee; thy throne shall be established forever" (II Samuel 7:12-16).

These words came from God to David after he had expressed his desire to build a temple for the Lord. David wanted to replace the temporary, portable tabernacle with a beautiful and permanent temple for the worship of God. His intentions and ambitions were certainly commendable, though God did not permit him to fulfill them. The covenant is confirmed by God in Psalm 89 which means it had not yet been fulfilled by that time.

Three specific promises of God to David stand out in this covenant. He would have a son, a posterity, called in the covenant his "seed." The "throne" of David was to be established forever. And finally, the "kingdom" of David was also to be established forever.

Three things were also promised to Solomon, David's son, in the covenant. He would be the one to build the temple which David has aspired to build. Solomon's throne, God promised, would also be established forever. The chastening hand of God, the covenant said, would come because of disobedience, yet the covenant would be fulfilled.

Again, the question must be asked, Has this covenant ever been fulfilled? If it has, how and in what sense has it been fulfilled? If it has not, will it ever be fulfilled, and if so, how will this become a reality? Christians are divided over their answers to these questions.

There is one more Biblical covenant which relates very much to things to come and needs to be considered.

The New Covenant

All who believe the Bible to be God's Word agree that God promised Israel a new covenant when He said to and through the prophet Jeremiah: "Behold, the days come, saith the Lord, that I will make a new covenant with the house of Israel, and with the house of Judah, Not according to the covenant that I made with their fathers in the day that I took them by the hand to bring them out of the land of Egypt, which, my covenant, they broke, although I was an husband unto them, saith the Lord; But this shall be the covenant that I will make with the house of Israel: After those days, saith the Lord, I will put my law in their inward parts, and write it in their hearts, and will be their God, and they shall be my people. And they shall teach no more every man his neighbour, and every man his brother, saying, Know the Lord; for they shall all know me, from the least of them unto the greatest of them, saith the Lord; for I will forgive their iniquity, and I will remember their sin no more" (Jeremiah 31:31-34).

Most important of all, the New Covenant assures Israel of a new heart. God's law will be written in the hearts of the people, was the promise (verse 33). Iniquity will be removed from the people. Their sin will be remembered no more (verse 34). The Holy Spirit of God, it is promised, will teach and find the people's hearts obedient and responsive (verse 34). Great material blessing will accompany Israel when she is brought into the land (Jeremiah 32:41). Hosea also speaks of an unprecedented outpouring of the favor and blessing of God (Hosea 2:19,20).

Several pressing questions confront the student of Scripture as he seeks to understand this covenant. To whom was the covenant given? Was it a conditional or an unconditional covenant? Has it ever been fulfilled? Does it await fulfillment in the future? How are we to understand the references to the new covenant in the New Testament?

Two Views of the Covenant

Premillennialists argue strongly that each of these four Biblical covenants is unconditional. That is, they believe the fulfillment of the covenants does not depend upon man's response but rather solely upon God. This does not mean, of course, that man's behavior and response to God in these covenants is not important. It does mean though that while man's obedience or disobedience affects his relation to the blessings of the covenants, yet his disobedience does not nullify or make void God's eternal covenants. God will do what He has promised! He will see to it that His Word is carried out!

Staunch defenders of the premillennial system speak at length of the unconditional nature of these covenants. John F. Walvoord argues that all of Israel's covenants were unconditional except one—the Mosaic. "The Abrahamic covenant is expressly declared to be eternal and therefore unconditional in numerous passages (Gen. 17:7,13,19; I Chron. 16:17; Ps. 105:10). The Palestinian covenant is likewise declared to be everlasting (Ezek. 16:60). The Davidic covenant is described in the same terms (2 Sam. 7:13,16,19; I Chron. 17:12; 22:10, Isa. 55:3; Ezek. 37:25). The new covenant with Israel is also eternal (Isa. 61:8; Jer. 32:40; 50:5; Heb. 13:20)."[19]

Altogether, Walvoord presents ten reasons for believing in the unconditional nature of the Abrahamic Covenant.[20]

Lewis Sperry Chafer, founder and first president of Dallas Theological Seminary and well known for his premillennialism, was very vocal in his belief that the four Biblical covenants were unconditional. Of the Palestinian Covenant in particular he said, "What is usually termed the Palestinian Covenant is the oft-repeated declaration by Jehovah, wholly unconditional, that the land which was promised to Abraham-'Unto thy seed have I given this land, from the river of Egypt unto the great river, the river Euphrates' (Gen. 15:18)—would be Abraham's possession forever. It is thus deeded to Abraham personally and becomes the legal inheritance of his posterity. On what other ground could it be styled 'the promised land'?"[21]

J. Dwight Pentecost, an articulate spokesman for premillennialism, argues similarly for the unconditional nature of the Davidic Covenant. He insists that it is called an eternal covenant (II Samuel 7:13) and therefore must rest for its fulfillment upon the faithfulness of God. Since the Davidic Covenant is primarily an expansion of the "seed" portion of the Abrahamic Covenant, it must be unconditional partaking of the same character as the original covenant. And furthermore, Pentecost argues, the reaffirmation of the Davidic Covenant after repeated acts of disobedience by Israel proves its unconditional nature.[22]

Charles C. Ryrie, another who champions the premillennial cause, also argues that all four of the Biblical covenants are unconditional in nature. Of the New Covenant he said, "The new covenant is an unconditional, grace covenant resting on the 'I will' of God. The frequency of the use of the phrase in Jeremiah 31:31-34 is striking. *Cf.* Ezekiel 16:26-62. The new covenant is an everlasting covenant. This is closely related to the fact that it is unconditional and made in grace."[23]

But that isn't all premillennialists believe about the Biblical covenants which relate to things to come. In addition to believing that they are all unconditional they also believe they were originally given to the people of Israel, not to the church. Furthermore, they insist that the national promises embodied in these covenants will therefore be realized by the nation to whom they were given. The national Jewish promises have not been, nor will they ever be, transferred to the church.

Ryrie is representative of normative premillennialism and is a recognized spokesman. Concerning the Abrahamic Covenant he said: "Does the Abrahamic covenant promise Israel a permanent existence as a nation? If it does, then the Church is not fulfilling Israel's promises, but rather Israel as a nation has a future yet in prospect; and does the Abrahamic covenant promise Israel permanent possession of the promised land? If it does, then Israel must yet come into possession of that land, for she has never fully possessed it in her history."[24]

"Israel means Israel and her promises have not been fulfilled by the Church. Since they have not, they must be fulfilled in the millennium if God's Word is not to be broken."[25]

So much for an overview of what premillennialists believe about the four Biblical covenants related to last things. But what do Christians of other persuasions believe about these same covenants?

The classic and the contemporary amillennial understanding of the covenants sees them all as either conditional in nature and thus abrogated because of Israel's disobedience or as transferred to "spiritual Israel," the church. Oswald T. Allis, who was a leading exponent of amillennialism, cites six reasons for believing the Abrahamic Covenant was conditional.[26]

It is sometimes difficult to understand exactly what amillennialists believe about the Biblical covenants. Sometimes it is contended that the covenants were conditional and therefore need not be fulfilled because Israel did not meet the conditions. And yet it is often said, sometimes by the same writers, that the covenants have been fulfilled historically in the Solomonic reign. And what is even more disconcerting is the amillennial argument that says the covenants are now being fulfilled by the church. Can all three of these things be true? They seem to contradict each other.

A contemporary convert from premillennialism to amillennial thinking said this about the Abrahamic Covenant: "Since the covenant was conditional, the contract is broken, and God is not bound to *Israel as a nation*. His covenant now is with the faithful remnant, and with the Gentile believers; these two groups constitute the Christian church, which today is the Israel of God (Gal. 6:16)."[27]

Of the New Covenant the same writer also said: "Although the covenant was made with Judah and Israel of the Old Testament, it was fulfilled in the spirtual Israel of the New Testament, that is, the church. Even this, however, was prophesied in scriptures such as Zechariah 2:11. Compare also Romans 15:8-12."[28]

Louis A. DeCaro, a recent amillennial writer, differs slightly with the traditional amillennial approach to the Abrahamic Covenant. He said, "The promise of land in the Abrahamic Covenant was historically fulfilled. That Israel lost it through disobedience is not chargeable to God. He gave ample warning through His servants, the prophets, that Israel would be dispossessed of the land if persistent in disobedience. The restoration after the Babylonian Captivity served the climactic purpose of the covenant—to bring Christ into the world. Since then, there is no more need for territoriality in the plan of God. There remains no more territorial fulfillment. The promise of seed found its immediate fulfillment in Old Testament Israel, the nation through which Jesus Christ came into the world. Christ, with the ultimate in the seed of Abraham, is the mediator of the covenant blessing. The proliferation of the seed continues in those who are united with Christ through faith in Him. In respect to Israel today, there is no national purpose remaining in the covenant which directly relates to the divine program of redemption. The claim of Israel today to Palestinian soil has no covenantal basis. The *de facto* existence of Israel today in Palestine is simply a secular Zionist attempt to fuse Judaism with statecraft. It is highly questionable whether this fusion of Judaism with statehood is related to either covenantal or prophetic thought."[29]

The postmillennial interpreters present a somewhat different view of the Biblical covenants from that expressed in the amillennial system though by no means agreeing with the premillenial school of thought.

For example, Loraine Boettner, a contemporary champion of the postmillennial faith, made this observation in his presentation and explanation of Scripture setting forth the New Covenant: "These are very great and precious promises, and certainly they point forward to conditions that have not yet been enjoyed on this earth. They are in fact so far-reaching and expansive that they stagger the imagination. Some amillennialists, finding no place in their system for these conditions, attempt to carry them over into the eternal state. But references to the 'nations' (Is. 2:2,4); judging the people with righteousness (Is. 65:20); etc., point unmistakably to this world."[30]

While in this way expressing his dissatisfaction with the amillennial interpretation of the covenants Boettner also revealed the same dissatisfaction with the premillennial views. "The promise given to Abraham that his seed should be very numerous and that through his seed all the nations of the earth should be blessed, finds its primary fulfillment, not in the totality of his physical descendants as at first sight would seem to have been indicated, nor even in the descendants through Jacob who stood in a special relationship to God, but in those who are his spiritual descendants (Gal. 3:7,29); and the seed through which all the nations of the earth were to be blessed was not his descendants in general, but one individual, which is Christ."[31]

The postmillennial view of the term "thousand years" in Revelation 20 and the possibility of Christ's literal reign from the throne of David reveals how the Biblical covenants are viewed. As expressed by J. Marcellus Kik: "The term *thousand years* in Revelation Twenty is a figurative expression used to describe the period of the Messianic Kingdom upon earth. It is that period from the first Advent of Christ until His Second Coming. It is the total or complete period of Christ's Kingdom upon earth."[32] Kik continues, "As a matter of fact there is not one text in the New Testament which speaks of Christ literally reigning upon earth in the literal city of Jerusalem. That is a teaching which is prevalent in some circles but is not taught by Christ or the apostles."[33]

Charles Hodge, a postmillennial theologian of years gone by, expressed a similar view of the Biblical covenants, a view not at all in harmony with premillennialism. In his presentation of arguments against the restoration of the Jews to the Holy Land he said among other things: "The idea that the Jews are to be restored to their own land and there constituted a distinct nation in the Christian Church is inconsistent not only with the distinct assertions of the Scriptures, but also with its plainest and most important doctrines."[34]

Why has so much attention been given to the Biblical covenants? That is a legitimate question. There are two reasons. First, these covenants are absolutely essential to one's view of things to come. No student of Scripture who wishes to present an eschatology—a teaching about things to come—can avoid them. They must be taken into account in deciding what things are yet to come. Secondly, and as a result of their importance to future things and their extensive revelation in the Bible, the covenants are a source of major difference among Christians. Christians "fight" about things to come because they disagree on the meanings of the Biblical covenants. And they disagree on the meanings because they follow different methods of interpretation.

Christians all agree that the fulfillment of prophecies provide strong evidence for the inspiration and authority of the Bible. Premillennial Christians go one step further and say the way in which prophecies have been fulfilled literally gives the believer warrant for saying the unfulfilled ones will indeed be fulfilled in the same way—literally. If this is not the case, the believer in the literal or normal interpretation of Scripture asks, Why?

[1] Bernard Ramm, *Protestant Biblical Interpretation* (Boston: W.A. Wilde Co., 1950), p. 1.

[2] Oswald T. Allis, *Prophecy and the Church* (Philadelphia: Presbyterian & Reformed Publishing Co., 1945), p. 238.

[3] William E. Cox, *Amillennialism Today* (Philadelphia: Presbyterian & Reformed Publishing Co., 1966), p. 13.

[4] Jay Adams, *The Time Is at Hand* (Nutley, New Jersey: The Presbyterian & Reformed Publishing Co., 1966), p. 8.

[5] Loraine Boettner, *The Millennium* (Philadelphia: Presbyterian & Reformed Publishing Co., 1964), p. 82.

[6] George N. H. Peters, *The Theocratic Kingdom* (Grand Rapids: Kregel Publications, 1957), p. 47.

[7] John F. Walvoord, *The Millennial Kingdom* (Findlay, Ohio: Dunham Publishing Co., 1959), p. 59.

[8] See Milton S. Terry, *Biblical Hermeneutics* (Grand Rapids: Zondervan Publishing House, 1969), pp. 163-174 for other methods.

[9] Bernard Ramm, *Protestant Biblical Interpretation* (Boston: W.A. Wilde Co., 1950), p. 53.

[10] *Ibid.*, p. 64.

[11] Examples of these may be found in J. Dwight Pentecost, *Things To Come* (Findlay, Ohio: Dunham Publishing Co., 1958), pp. 9-15 and Paul Lee Tan, *The Interpretation of Prophecy* (Winona Lake, Indiana: BMH Books, Inc., 1974), pp. 29-39.

[12] Charles C. Ryrie, *Dispensationalism Today* (Chicago: Moody Press, 1965), pp. 87,88.

[13] Allis, *op. cit.,* p. 17.

[14] *Ibid.*, pp. 17, 18.

[15] Pentecost, *op. cit.*, pp. 14,15.

[16] Ramm, *op. cit.*, p. 23.

[17] *Ibid.*, p. 21.

[18] See Menno J. Brunk, *Fulfilled Prophecies* (Crockett, Kentucky: Rod and Staff Publishing, Inc., 1971).

[19] Walvoord, *op. cit.*, p. 150.

[20] *Ibid.*, pp. 150-52.

[21] Lewis Sperry Chafer, *Systematic Theology* (Dallas: Dallas Seminary Press, 1948), IV, 317.

[22] Pentecost, *op. cit.*, p. 104.

[23] Ryrie, *The Basis of the Premillennial Faith* (New York: Loizeaux Brothers, 1953), p. 112.

[24] *Ibid.*, pp. 48,49.

[25] *Ibid.*, p. 125.

[26] Allis, *op. cit.*, pp. 32-36.

[27] Cox, *Biblical Studies in Final Things* (Philadelphia: Presbyterian & Reformed Publishing Co., 1967), p. 7.

[28] *Ibid.*, p. 8.

[29] Louis A. DeCaro, *Israel Today: Fulfillment of Prophecy?* (Philadelphia: Presbyterian & Reformed Publishing Co., 1974), pp. 64,65.

[30] Boettner, *op. cit.*, p. 123.

[31] *Ibid.*, pp. 102,103.

[32] J. Marcellus Kik, *Revelation Twenty—An Exposition* (Philadelphia: Presbyterian & Reformed Publishing Co., 1955), p. 29.

[33] *Ibid.*, pp. 45,46.

[34] Charles Hodge, *Systematic Theology* (Grand Rapids: Wm. B. Eerdmans Publishing Co., 1968), III, 810.

CHAPTER 5

Fighting
About the Future

The fight is on! Christians are at war, and it is not all being fought against Satan and sin. God's people, unfortunately, are engaged in conflicts among themselves and with each other. The conflicts cannot always be called cold wars. Sometimes they get very heated. One of the major areas of debate concerns fighting about the future—differences over views of things to come.

Why are these differences so important? Really now, what difference does it make whether a Christian believes there will be a future earthly kingdom of peace or whether he does not believe it? Is it important to distinguish between the so-called rapture of the church and the second coming of Christ? Does it matter all that much? Who cares whether Christ, the church, or civil powers establish the kingdom if, in fact, it is ever established? And if the earthly kingdom of universal peace and righteousness does come, when will this be? Is not the important thing that Christ will come again to this earth and usher His own into the eternal state? In short, who, who cares whether there is going to be a kingdom on earth or not? To be with Christ is most important and the far better thing, isn't it? Why even argue at all for a particular view and order of things to come?

Some have described their view of the kingdom and related events as "pan millennialism"—everything will pan out all right in the end. Unfortunately, too many Bible believers share such a view regarding the future.

Let's retrace our steps before we journey any further. We have set forth reason for another book on prophecy. We don't need another defense of a particular view of the future and certainly not a new view. What we do need is a better understanding of the divergent views, and a better understanding among those who hold divergent views. Our eyes need to be lifted beyond our differences over last things to the many things we evangelicals hold in common.

The major events of the future which evangelicals all accept were presented in the first chapter. In chapter two the different views of the order of future events were given. There we reviewed differences over what will take place when Christ returns and what relation the church will have to any future great tribulation.

In the preceding chapter the question, "Why all these differences?" was before us. Our conclusion was, the differences exist because two different methods of Biblical interpretation are used. Some seek to follow a consistently literal, normal approach in their interpretation of all Scripture, including all unfulfilled prophecy. Others do not believe it is possible to do this. They believe they are justified in using a less than literal approach when it comes to some unfulfilled prophecy.

We come now to that part of our discussion when the reality of the conflict over what lies ahead must be set forth. It must be admitted, evangelical Christians are at odds with each other over God's plan for the future. In fact, they are at war over things to come. And the battle hasn't just started. It has been going on for a long, long time, though it has been intensified lately.

A number of things have contributed to stepping up the action. Perhaps the most significant one has been the recent popularity given the premillennial, pretribulational view. This has come through books such as Hal Lindsey's *Late Great Planet Earth*, Ken Taylor's *The Living Bible*, and others. This is admitted by those who oppose pretribulationism. "The present popularity of pretribulationism is due largely to the widespread use of the Scofield Bible (detailed in the editor's notes), and the many recent authors such as Dwight Pentecost, John Walvoord, E. Schuyler English, and William Pettingill. Many evangelical publishing houses, periodicals, seminaries, Bible schools, faith missions, and popular Bible radio teachers are responsible for its continuing presentation along with many prophetic films and charts, conferences, gospel songs, and a host of recently published paperback books, such as *The Late, Great Planet Earth*."[1]

Whatever the reason, Christians, members of the same heavenly family, are engaged in a nasty fight with each other over last things. Refusing to admit it will not change things. We may not want the people of the world to know about our struggles and conflicts but they do anyway. Great shame and disgrace already has been brought to the cause of Christ by us.

The evidence of the fight is overwhelming. I will try not to labor the point, but I must tell it like it is. The purpose in giving these facts is to arouse the reader to the reality of the fight so that he can be a part of easing the tensions. What I present here does not thrill me; it tears at my heart.

WHO STARTED THE FIGHT?

That is a good question! Who will admit they started it? To ask this question of Christians in the struggle over the future is almost like asking the two neighborhood boys who started the fight which left them both with bloody noses. He did. No, he did. The accusations go on and on and on.

I am not sure much would be gained even if we were sure just who started the fight. About all it would do, at best, would be to give the one side cause for more accusation against the other side.

The truth that cannot be denied is, there is a fight. We can call it something nicer if we want to, but that won't change a thing. A difference of opinion is one thing. But an angry warfare with those who hold a different viewpoint, involving a bitter suspicious attitude, is something else.

The fact is that soon after the apostles passed from the earthly scene, differences developed over end times. The battle has raged among evangelicals at least since the third century A.D. In recent years the presence of Israel as a nation in the very geographic area promised to her has added fuel to the fire. The premillennialists point to this phenomenon and say, "I told you so." The amillennialists and post millennialists respond vigorously by saying the nation as a political entity and its presence in the holy land have absolutely nothing to do with the fulfillment of prophecy.[2]

WHO IS DOING THE FIGHTING?

The theologians, educators, authors, and preachers have wielded the weapons. Lay people in the pew are usually given the viewpoint espoused by the particular person giving the information or the organization with which he is affiliated. And of course that is understandable. We expect to have a person promote the cause he embraces and thinks is right rather than some other one.

So what it amounts to is a fight among the top brass. The evangelical leaders of the people can't agree among themselves. But the conflict doesn't stop there, though that is where it started. Because of the popularity of religion today, and even of Christianity, and in particular the premillennial pretribulational views, lay folks are also becoming involved in the struggle. The average Christian is reading more than he used to. The Christian publishing houses continue to turn out hundreds of books and material on prophecy. The news media includes more information of Biblical truth than it did even a few years ago.

As a result of the popularity of the teaching of a rapture of the church before the great tribulation, the coming man of sin, a world religion and government, and other similar things, the ordinary person is getting a view of the future and is sharing it with his friends. And as a result, differences erupt and the fight of the professionals becomes a fight among the people in the pews as well.

HOW GOES THE BATTLE?

The furor over the future is a battle of words. But back of the biting words there are attitudes and feelings which reflect strong deep-seated differences.

When strong differences are expressed, each side inevitably accuses the other side of being unfair and of misrepresenting its view. That's the way it is among evangelicals with differing views of God's program for the future. Understandably, it is difficult to present an opposing view as anything less than erroneous when you feel strongly that yours is the true view.

It is to be understood that objections will be raised by opposing sides of an issue. Honest differences will always exist as long as there are two people around. But the differences and disagreements develop into open warfare when slander of people and views, unsupportable accusations, judgment of motives, name calling, and insinuations which raise suspicions are used of those with whom we differ. When this happens, Christian principles are thrown to the wind. Carnality then rules the day. The works of the flesh, not the fruit of the Spirit, are manifest when honest differences on an issue such as eschatology cannot be expressed without the smell of gun fire and below-the-belt blows. Views of the future program of God are often presented as though those who hold differing views could not possibly be evangelical and are less than sincere in their attempt to understand God's Word.

Adherents of each of the views of future happenings set forth in chapter 2 are guilty of unfairness. All the bullets have not been fired from the guns of one particular side. This does not mean everyone who has ever said anything in defense of his view of things to come has been guilty of fighting unfairly. Many disagree without being disagreeable. Unfortunately, though, there have been a number of those who sought to set forth and defend a particular viewpoint who have engaged in tactics which have not been fair to their opponents or honoring to Christ.

Some of the evidence I will now cite reveals the intensity of the fight over things to come from the past but much of it is from the present.

A view from the anti-premillennial side

Critics of pretribulationism and dispensationalism have frequently engaged in attacks upon personalities who have been active in the rise and spread of these points of view.[3] Attacks upon people have been used, it appears, to discredit the positions they hold.

The guilt by association tactic is sometimes used in the discussion of prophecy. One writer compared dispensationalism with destructive higher criticism of the Bible: "Dispensationalism shares with higher criticism its fundamental error . . . . In a word, despite all their differences, higher criticism and dispensationalism are in this one respect strikingly similar. Higher criticism divides the Scriptures up into documents which differ from or contradict one another. Dispensationalists divide the Bible up into dispensations which differ from and even contradict one another . . . ."[4]

The same writer also implies some relation between Russellism (Jehovah's Witness teaching) and premillennialism because both accept the Abrahamic Covenant as unconditional in nature.[5]

Dispensationalists are said to have "actual contempt for the thinking of historic Christian theology."[6] They engage in "arbitrary and reckless division of the Bible into three compartments."[7] Dispensationalism itself is termed a "heresy" by some nondispensational writers. "Carnal theories" are said to be a part of dispensationalism.

In his classic defense of posttribulationism Alexander Reese leveled his attacks upon pretribulationism with fiery words. Others have caught the tenor of his criticisms in these words: "Mr. Reese does not seem to have made up his mind whether those whom he attacks so trenchantly are fools, or only knaves; his language, indeed, frequently suggests that they are both! Here are some things he says about them, taken at random as the pages are turned: They are guilty of 'aggressive sophistry and fantastic exegesis,' and of 'paltry reasoning.' They prefer 'any rubbish to the true and obvious explanation' of passage, and they 'wrest the Scriptures.' Their preference for the line of teaching they favor is 'no longer a question of exegesis . . . It is simply a question of ethics. . . . Have we the right moral disposition toward the truth, or will we still cling to error . . . shall we act against the truth or for the truth?' . . . They are not God-fearing readers of the Bible, but 'theorists,' 'showing little acquaintance with great exegesis.' Their teaching is 'consistent and ludicrous' in its 'absurdity.' Its effect is to blight 'Bible study and Christian fellowship all over the world.' 'It has cursed the [Brethren] movement from the beginning.' 'They wrote their errors on their broad phylacteries.' . . . They 'are misguided and misleading teachers.' And, indeed, 'Paul informs us that they were *false* teachers who taught thus.'"[8]

Pretribulationists are said to appeal to "unworthy motives." They want to escape the coming tribulation because they are afraid of it. "Unworthy and selfish impulses" make Christians appeal to the view. Those who believe the church will not go through the coming tribulation have a strain of "weak-kneed, invertebrate, spineless sentiment."

Premillennialists are said to deal "rashly" with Scripture. Their position is said to be typical of the wilderness experience of Israel and the amillennial view is typified as the land of Canaan. One passage of Scripture is "superimposed" on another passage. Scripture passages are wedded together in unnatural ways.

Those who subscribe to the premillennial view have a "disease" called "exegetical diplopia, i.e., double vision," in the thinking of one critic. He views the belief of his brethren as "the bifurcated and diplopic premillennial scheme." They are accused of "an artificial interpretation invented to circumvent the clear intent of the passage."

Pretribulationism is said to have "directly and indirectly caused the deaths of thousands—perhaps millions—of persons." Such a bold statement was made because pretribulationists did not encourage Chinese Christians to leave their country before the Communist take-over.

Premillennialists and pretribulationists "turn heaven and earth upside down in order to win one convert to their school of thought." And, "they make this one belief a test of Christian fellowship." They take the "glory which ought to go to Christ and give it to the non-believing nation of Israel."

Frequently, dispensationalists have been accused of

believing in more than one way of salvation, although they have cited reasons why they believe in one way of salvation for all time.[9] Their opponents still persist in leveling the charge notwithstanding the evidence to the contrary.[10]

Interpretations given by premillennialists are said to be "symptomatic of dispensationalism's penchant for making unwarranted distinctions and dichotomies." Belief in national promises yet to be fulfilled in Israel "is a dispensational concoction and is not at all implied in Scripture."

"The Millennium-Rapture Hoax" is the bold title of a tract intended to show that belief in a rapture of the church and a future earthly millennium is a hoax. It is a doctrine "spun out of this air." The rapture theory is "false" and an "erroneous belief."

"Millennialism is incompatible with the very nature of faith," wrote one critic. It, in fact, is "dangerous to the Christian faith." Another said it is a "fantasy" which even endangers a Christian's salvation. "Millennialism is one of the anti-scriptural teachings held by a good number of conservatives."

Dispensationalism is sometimes called an "errant scheme" promoting a desire for things to come "with little desire for the knowledge of holiness."

A view from the premillennial side

Is the fight all one-sided? Are the opponents of premillennialism and pretribulationism the only ones who engage in slander and the smear attack approach? Are they the only ones really fighting in this battle among evangelicals over things to come? From the above, the reader may suppose that is what I am trying to say. No, there is blame on the doorsteps of premillennialists and pretribulationists also.

Historically, premillennialism has been set forth as a unified system of theology. There is no lack of of material written in defense of premillennialism, dispensationalism, or pretribulationism. But the same cannot be said for the other views of last things. The proponents of these have been mostly involved in attacking the premillennial scheme of events. Jay Adams, an amillennialist or, as he prefers to be called, a realized millennialist, candidly admitted this of the view he embraces in his book *The Time Is at Hand:* "Most recent amillennial publications have been largely negative in approach."[11] He also said amillennialists "have conceived of their task as almost wholly negative (that is, it consists merely in proving the premillennialist wrong)."[12]

Because they have been primarily involved in attacking the premillennial system, it is understandable that we may find more evidence of the fight from its opponents. On the other hand, since premillennial pretribulationists have been more engaged in setting forth a positive declaration and defense of their position than they have in opposing their opponents, we would expect to find less of the kind of thing noted above.

But by no means does this mean premillennialists have not made their contribution to the battle. They have! Just as not all who reject premillennial pretribulationism are guilty of the above charges, so not all proponents of the view may be legitimately charged with the following. However, all need take special precaution to avoid these dangers.

First, what I call overstatements of the position have been made. I mean by this, broad, sweeping, all-inclusive statements which simply cannot be supported. The premillennial enthusiasts need to be careful about making generalizations.

This error is perhaps most evident when it comes to the matter of hermeneutics. As we have seen, premillennialists follow the literal or normal method. But often, when saying this and contrasting themselves with amillennialists, premillennialists give the impression that their opponents never employ the literal method. And, of course, this simply is not true. Even some of the prophecies of the Bible are interpreted literally by amillenarians. They do not always use the allegorical method. In interpreting most of Scripture, in fact, evangelical amillennialists and postmillennialists use the very same method of interpretation used by the premillennialists. It is only in the understanding of certain unfulfilled prophecies that a less than literal approach is followed.

William Cox in his defense of amillennialism accuses John F. Walvoord, one of the most ardent defenders of premillennialism, of this very thing. He quotes the following from Walvoord: "Premillenarians follow the so-called 'grammatical historical' literal interpretation while amillenarians use a spiritualizing method." [13] After pointing out that Walvoord later did in fact admit that amillennialists do not interpret all Scripture allegorically, Cox accused him of double talk. [14]

There are other areas where premillennialists have overstated their case. Sometimes in explaining a passage of Scripture or when referring to those holding variant views, it is done. It is easy to say, "Scripture always teaches," or "Nowhere does the Bible say," or "The church is never called or referred to as . . . ." The same applies to references to individuals. Statements such as, "all amillennialists," or "all posttribulationists," or "no amillennialist or posttribulationist ever . . ." are much too sweeping.

Second, the guilt by association technique has been used by premillennarians. Again, this error usually comes up when the important subject of hermeneutics is discussed.

True to fact, there are few, if any, theologically liberal premillennarians. This is so because they follow the literal method of interpreting all the Bible. It is also true that theological liberals and Roman Catholics embrace amillennialism. The same method used by evangelical amillennialism in interpreting certain prophetic Scripture is used by theological liberals and Roman Catholics freely throughout Scripture. When this is done, of course, the cardinal doctrines of the faith are rejected. It is true, the literal method when consistently used is a great obstacle to liberal theology and Roman Catholic theology.[15] But by no means are all who do not thus use it thereby liberal or Roman Catholic.

Guilt by association is also often applied when pecularities of a particular person are attributed to all who share his basic view. There are, as we have noted, significant variations within amillennialism, postmillennialism, and posttribulation. An alleged error or overstatement of one person must not be charged to all in his eschatological camp. Neither should a minority view be attributed to the majority.

Third, there have been times when premillennialists have left bad insinuations by the way they have presented their case. Sometimes what is left unsaid is more damaging than what is said.

I believe it would be very easy for many readers to get the impression from some premillennial and pretribulational writing that those not holding that position are really less than honest. Insinuations of dishonesty and purposeful misrepresentations are sometimes left by the way things are presented.

Too, the way the premillennial, pretribulational position is stated and explained by some, it would be easy to believe all who disagree with it could not possibly be evangelical.

I have taught in the college and seminary classroom for fourteen years. It has always been true, and I still find it so, that students are often shocked to learn that there are amillennialists and postmillennialists who are thoroughly evangelical. Somehow, they sometimes do not get that from the things they hear and read. That lack of knowledge, in the long run, really adds fuel to the fire of opposition. Some of the greatest Bible commentaries, devotional books, and theology books have been and still are authored by those who are not premillennial or pretribulational. Great men of God do not all accept the same view of things to come.

Not a few pretribulationists leave the impression they have all the answers to all the problems of the future. An attitude of pride comes through what they say and write. They give the impression that their view has no problems. Some are even bold to pronounce in areas where angels fear to tread.

For example, Israel's existence as a nation on May 14, 1948 and her occupancy of the city of Jerusalem in 1967 have resulted in unneccessary dogmatism about the future.[16]

Frequently, one hears or reads the premillennial pretribulational view expressed as though the opposition doesn't have even a basic grasp of Scripture. In short, the opponents are sometimes made to look like Biblical imbecils. Statements like these give this impression: "Even a cursory reading of the passage . . ." "The simple reading of the passage makes this meaning apparent." "Dedicated students of the Bible know . . ." "The premillennial view is clearly taught throughout Scripture."

I do not want to judge the motives of anyone engaged in the struggle described above. Many times those who make strong statements against their opponents or in defense of their own position do not mean them as they are understood. But, whether or not unchristian attitudes exist or harm is intended, what is said often does grave injury to others and to the cause of Christ. Great care must be exercised, therefore, in how viewpoints are expressed lest our differences degenerate into bitter all-out warfare.

There simply is no place in the family of God for name calling, false accusations, slander, evil insinuations, and the guilty-by-association technique. God forgive us all of such sins!

[1] Arthur D. Katterjohn, *The Rapture—When?* (Wheaton: Arthur D. Katterjohn, 220 East Union, 1975), p. 60.

[2] Louis A. DeCaro, *Israel Today: Fulfillment of Prophecy?* (Philadelphia: Presbyterian & Reformed Publishing Co., 1974). This entire volume presents this thesis.

[3] See, for example, Oswald T. Allis, *Prophecy and the Church* (Philadelphia: Presbyterian and Reformed Publishing Co. 1945); William E. Cox, *An Examination of Dispensationalism* (Philadelphia: Presbyterian & Reformed Publishing Co., 1963); Clarence B. Bass, *Backgrounds to Dispensationalism* (Grand Rapids: Eerdmans Publishing Co., 1960); C. Norman Kraus, *Drop in America* (Richmond, Virginia: John Knox Press, 1958); and the writings of Dave MacPherson (Kansas City, Mo.: Heart of America Bible Society).

[4] Allis, "Modern Dispensationalism and the Doctrine of the Unity of the Scriptures," *The Evangelical Quarterly,* 8 (January, 1936), 24.

[5] Allis, *Prophecy and the Church,* p. 48.

[6] Cox, *op. cit.,* p. 3.

[7] *Ibid.*

[8] C. F. Hogg and W. E. Vine, *The Church and the Tribulation* (London: Pickering & Inglis LTD., [n.d.]), p. 11.

[9] Charles C. Ryrie, *Dispensationalism Today* (Chicago: Moody Press, 1965), pp. 110-31.

[10] See Daniel Payton Fuller, "The Hermeneutics of Dispensationalism" (unpublished Doctor's dissertation, Northern Baptist Theological Seminary, Chicago, 1957) and also Cox, *op.cit.,* p. 17f. for examples.

[11] Jay E. Adams, *The Time Is at Hand* (Philadelphia: Presbyterian & Reformed Publishing Co, 1974), p. VII.

[12] *Ibid.,* p. 7.

[13] Cox, *Amillennialism Today* (Philadelphia: Presbyterian & Reformed Publishing Co, 1966), p. 15 quoting from John F. Walvoord, *The Millennial Kingdom* (Findlay, Ohio: Dunham Publishing Co., 1959), p. 59.

[14] Cox, *op. cit.,* pp. 15,16.

[15] Alva J. McClain, *The Greatness of the Kingdom* (Chicago: Moody Press, 1968), pp. 139-46; Paul Lee Tan, *The Interpretation*

of Prophecy (Winona Lake, Indiana: B.M.H. Books, 1974), pp. 275-77; and Walvoord, *op. cit.*, pp. 3-17.

[16] See an example of this in Hal Lindsey, *The Late Great Planet Earth* (Grand Rapids: Zondervan, 1970). In broad outline this book represents the pretribulational position, but not all who embrace the view share Lindsey's dogmatism in areas.

CHAPTER 6

Why the Fighting
Continues

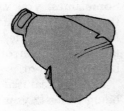

As noted in the previous chapter, the debates which theologians, educators, and preachers have over the issues of the order of future events have filtered down to the lay people. On the professional level there is a certain kind of fight over things to come, and the basic reason for it is one of hermeneutics—the method of interpretation used. But on the nonprofessional level there are many more reasons why the fighting continues.

Of course, these two levels are not altogether isolated, the one from the other. Many times, those we have chosen to refer to as professionals are tenacious in their beliefs for the very same reason the nonprofessionals are. So, while certain unfulfilled prophecy has, in fact, been put in the ring by the professionals, the people watching the fight have also gotten involved. And by the same token, even though the question of how to interpret Scripture is very basic to the conflict, many other reasons for the fighting enter in.

The purpose of this chapter is to name some of these additional reasons and to discuss them briefly. Some of them are more important than others, but all of them are a part of the reason why evangelicals keep unfulfilled prophecy in the ring.

The fight has been going on for a long time. Neither side has been willing to concede much of anything. And so it goes, round after round. When those in the ring are too weak to keep fighting, they are quickly replaced by others who carry on the struggle. Some of the contestants are not very Christian in their behavior, as we have seen. Sometimes, you would hardly know another member of the body of Christ is in the ring with them. As you watch from the sidelines, you hardly avoid being affected and involved. The strong points and weak points of each side become evident.

But the real issues are not clear. Are these people really being honest? you ask. When you talk about the different viewpoints with others in the grandstand, you soon find yourself taking sides, and before you know it, you realize you are arguing with your best friend. Bad feelings soon develop and soon you find yourself with a circle of friends who share your views, or at least most of them.

SOME REASONS WHY EVANGELICALS DIFFER

Hermeneutics, as has been noted, is without question the most basic reason for the fight. But what are some other reasons? Without any particular importance in the order in which these appear, here are some things which I believe keep the conflict raging.

Traditionalism

None of the major creeds of the church include premillennialism in their statements. Those who place much emphasis upon church creeds and traditional beliefs find it difficult to embrace a view not included in the beliefs of the ancients. That is understandable.

The danger to be avoided here is that of equating the creed or traditional belief with the Bible. This is sometimes done. The question is, Does the creed, indeed, restate what the Bible teaches? Only the Bible is inspired of God and therefore divinely authoritative. Therefore in the final analysis, Scripture must be our first and most basic creed.

In the history of Biblical doctrine eschatology, the study of last things, came in last for discussion. First, the ancient church fathers studied and formulated doctrinal statements in the doctrines of Scripture, God the Father, God the Son, God the Holy Spirit, sin, salvation, and the church. Only sometime after the Reformation was there any lengthy and specific concentration on things to come. So one looks in vain for definitive statements regarding any or the various systems or eschatology in the doctrinal formulations of the ancient ecumenical councils of the church. The Person and work of Christ were chief concerns of the early church fathers, not a well defined order of events in connection with His second coming.

The fighting over unfulfilled prophecies continues because some Christians place more emphasis and importance upon ancient beliefs and crucial statements than others do.

Relation to Other Truths

Serious students of Scripture know that the way they understand God's plan and program for the future bears upon a number of related matters in God's Word. Other Biblical teaching relates directly to the doctrine of last things. For example, one's view of unfulfilled prophecy, if he is consistent, will determine his view of certain things about the church and Israel and vice versa. Much of the Old Testament and the New will be understood differently according to the particular view of future events one embraces.

Because these relationships between Biblical truth exist, it is very natural for people to be reluctant to change. To give up a certain view of things to come in place of another view means other areas of doctrine need to be restudied too.

Even the present daily Christian life is affected by one's understanding of God's calendar of future events. Arthur D. Katterjohn, who believes the church will go through the coming great tribulation, highlighted the importance of future things to present experiences: "Does the church of today face the intensifying of sin and lawlessness, resulting ultimately in the revelation of sin (Antichrist) and his persecution of the church to a degree never before experienced, before we are gathered together unto Jesus Christ at His return? Or . . . are we to look for the Rapture—that secret and imminent catching away of the church to heaven before that time of tribulation? Your answer to the above question has a great bearing upon your activities as a Christian in the next few years. If the first alternative is indeed correct, then we must teach that the church is to prepare for that great persecution, making haste in the light of the present-day fulfillment of prophecies and the increasing decadence of mankind and his way of life."[1]

Current World Events

The crisis times in which we live draw attention to what the Bible has to say about the future. Naturally as man's attention is drawn to the unfulfilled prophecies of Scripture and he learns of various views of those prophecies, sides will be taken and tension will mount.

In 1948 the state of Israel was formed. In 1967 during the Six-day War Israel occupied all of the city of Jerusalem. Russia and China have become world powers to be reckoned with. The world is threatened by famine.

World powers have it in their power to destroy each other. And we could go on and on naming things which have made men's hearts fail them for fear.

Because of what is going on in the world the Christian public, and even many of the unsaved, are beginning to turn to the Bible for answers. They find that much of what is taking place in the world seems to parallel predictions of Scripture. Then they discover the differences which prevail over exactly what the Bible teaches about the future. While God's Word is clear in its teaching about certain crucial events in the future, it is not always as clear in the specifics and the order in which the events will unfold. In other words, there are areas of prophecy which are not spelled out in a particular passage leaving no room for different interpretations. Various passages and issues must be brought together. Pieces of the eschatological puzzle must be put together. But not all Christians see the pieces in the same way. Some of the pieces appear to fit in more than one place. And some of the pieces are often forced and made to fit even though they really don't. Thus, the conflict continues.

Stubbornness

Nobody will want to admit that he just may have in him a streak of what was called in my neighborhood when I was a boy, "bullheadedness." Today a person who has the same characteristics we say is opinionated. Now a certain amount of that kind of thing, properly distributed, has its place. But when we refuse to even hear the other side or admit areas of weakness in our own position, we have put on the boxing gloves. We have stepped inside the ring, and what is more, have probably made up our minds to stay there as long as we live.

A number of reasons for this unchristian attitude could be cited. Maybe we are kind of stubborn-like in other areas of our lives too. If things aren't the way we think

105

they should be, do we think they are all wrong? Are we willing to change our ideas or our ways when it's obvious that a change is for the better?

Prejudice

Could it be that we are so prejudiced that we can't look at our view objectively? By and large, people believe what they have been taught. There are exceptions, of course, but usually what we have been taught and what we have read most of so conditions us that with a few modifications we embrace those views. And then after we have believed those things, shared them with others, and perhaps identified ourselves with the view and those who hold it, a change does not come easy. Who of us enjoys admitting he is wrong?

And therefore, the fight continues. Come what may, we are what we are and nobody or no amount of information will make us change our view. Now, isn't that really about the way it is? It is unfortunate that we are that way, but that doesn't change the facts. That simply is the way people are, even Christian people!

Insufficient Information

This reason of not having sufficient information will be hard for some to acknowledge. Not necessarily through any fault of their own, large numbers of lay people, nonprofessionals, have only a sparse knowledge of why they believe what they believe or at least what their church or pastor believes. Generally speaking, people leave doctrinal beliefs up to the clergy. If they like a church and/or have been reared in it, they give general consent to its teaching, especially in areas of future things, and accept them without question. Generally speaking, lay people do not bother to examine the theological beliefs of their church, especially after they join.

It would be interesting indeed to ask an average group

of Christian people from a variety of churches what they themselves believe about the future and why they believe it. Could it be that much of the hassle over God's future program for the world and many a round in the fight could be eliminated if Christians would really seek to understand why they believe what they say they believe? If we don't think we have the time or don't have the interest to study out our beliefs, then at least we should not be quite as dogmatic and be less judgmental and condemnatory of those with differing viewpoints.

Selfishness

Can we face the thought that it is not unusual for some to promote a certain view because it gives them the leader image? They enjoy holding a view that is somewhat unique in the circles. And naturally there will always be numbers of people who will be followers. Such people seem to enjoy rabble rousing when they and their cause become popular.

Quite often, such a spirit is also associated with an attitude of dogmatism. Certain personalities seem to have such a bent to them. Some people feel that they must be right on everything. They cannot tolerate any ambiguity or uncertainty. All things for them are always either black or white, yes or no. Never is there any place for the gray, the uncertain.

Spiritual Pride

Whenever we feel we have a corner on God's truth, we give evidence of spiritual pride. It is foolish to think we have all the answers or that our view is free of all problems. And yet how often we become selfish and proud in our view of what God is going to do in the future. Often, we fight with other members of the family of God because we are sinfully selfish and proud.

Escapist Mentality

After talking to numbers of people over a number of

years, I have come to believe that many believe the church will be delivered from the future seven-year tribulation because they can't imagine enduring the horrors of it. They don't believe they will be in it simply because they want to escape it. And who wouldn't want to escape it? Yet, it must be realized that some saints of God will be in that awful time of unprecedented trouble.

Martyr Complex

Strong feelings of desire to be absent during the future outpouring of God's wrath leads to quarrels with those who don't believe the church will escape that awful time.

The martyr complex is another thing which keeps the fighting going. While some Christians wilt when they think of the future tribulation, others, often with pride, say they will be happy to suffer for Christ through that time. Often those who boast of willingness to die for Christ look askance upon those who want to be delivered from the tribulation. Both of these attitudes often serve to divide the body of Christ.

Overstatements and Misrepresentations

Starting with the professionals who represent all the various views of things to come, I have found broad sweeping statements which have caused argument. One's zeal and enthusiasm must be harnassed so that they do not lead to erroneous statements.

When the professionals are guilty of overstatements and misrepresentations, it is not surprising to find the same coming from the laity. Without intending to misrepresent, that is often exactly what results. Too many times what is claimed for a particular view is really not true to the facts. Half truths, unwarranted dogmatism, and incomplete presentations only add fuel to a fire that is already too hot and has been burning too long.

Honest Exegetical Problems

If the Bible was as clear in its teaching of the details and order of events for the future as it is on what a man must do to be saved, there would be less room for different views on the subject. But God in His wisdom has not seen fit to present all truth in the same way and to the same extent. Some things He has chosen to give us in broad outline and with less emphasis upon the specific details.

We are responsible, though, for all God's truth. When it speaks on matters essential to the faith such as the deity of Christ, His vicarious atonement, man's total inability to merit favor with God, and the total authority of Scripture, evangelicals must not and do not differ. But there is room for difference over how some of the unfulfilled prophecies will be fulfilled. This is true simply because there are passages of Scripture which when taken by themselves may be legitimately used to support differing points of view.[2] All the Scriptural evidence is not on the side of one particular view.

Semantics

Webster defines semantics as "the branch of linguistics concerned with the nature, structure, and especially the development and changes, of the meanings of speech forms."

I believe the fighting over the future continues partly because not everybody means the same thing by the words they use. There are terms like "kingdom," "second coming," "return of the Lord," "dispensation," "literal," which mean different things to different people. These need to be defined and understood carefully. If they are not, needless conflicts will arise. We must not be quick to assume what is meant when words with different usages and meanings are used.

Straw Men

By a straw man in this context I mean a view not really held by the one to whom it is assigned. Literature in defense of the various evangelical views of future things frequently includes straw men. A certain belief is said to be held by those who embrace a particular view of eschatology. Sometimes the belief is terribly misstated and other times not at all common or peculiar to the position being criticized. But when these straw men appear in print or are preached from pulpits and taught in classrooms, they are soon so closely associated with the view that they become genuine bones of contention among God's people.

Doubtless, there are other things which serve to continue the fighting about the future. The ones listed above have come to my attention as I have examined my own heart and head and the literature on all sides and have talked with a cross section of evangelicals.

What can we do to change the situation? We can withdraw from the battle. The least we can and should do is take a long hard look at ourselves and our attitudes. Are we disagreeing with our brothers and sisters in Christ in a spirit of Christian love and respect for them? Does genuine honesty mark our response to God's Word and His people? Is our particular view based upon what we really believe the Bible teaches or is it just the party line we are parroting? Let's do our best to be a part of the solution and not a part of the problem as we talk about things to come.

NOTES FOR CHAPTER 6

[1] Arthur D. Katterjohn, *The Rapture—When?* (Wheaton: Arthur D. Katterjohn, 220 East Union, 1975), p. 1.

[2] Robert H. Gundry in his book, *The Church and the Tribulation* (Grand Rapids: Zondervan, 1973) illustrates this numbers of times by showing how certain passages may be used to support both pre and posttribulationism and are not determinative in themselves.

CHAPTER 7

Let's Take Prophecy
Out of the Ring

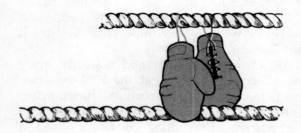

There is no question about it—prophecy is in the ring. The ancient bout has been and still is with fellow believers and has resulted in a lot of bloody noses, black eyes, and even some broken bones. Serious injury has come and almost irreparable harm done to the body of Christ as a result of the conflict. Some of God's people seem to keep their gloves on all the time. Always on the alert, they wait for every possible opportunity to go another round in the ring. Sometimes they make the opportunity if none seems to be forthcoming.

Sincerely and with all seriousness, I would like to plead with my brothers in Christ to join me in taking prophecy out of the ring. The fight has accomplished little for good. I can't believe God has been or is now pleased with the fight viewed from the gallery of heaven.

May I make these suggestions in connection with my appeal?

SUGGESTIONS FOR SOLUTION

Have Convictions

I believe strongly that God's people ought to have convictions regarding future things. This applies to both those we have referred to as the professionals and to the nonprofessionals. What one believes about unfulfilled prophecy is very important. I have not been saying that everything other than belief in the second coming, future resurrection and judgment and eternity is peripheral. Everything in God's Word is very important. Nothing is peripheral with God.

As a part of Christian growth and maturity every believer ought to grapple with what the Bible teaches, including what it teaches about the future. Honest effort should put forth to correlate Scripture and to see it all fitting into a pattern. Everything in God's Word is important and that includes unfulfilled prophecy, all of it. It is highly important that we understand as best we can what lies in store for us as individuals, the church, and for the world in general.

A good number of unfulfilled prophecies of future events are very clear in Scripture. As we have seen, evangelicals all agree on these. But what should we do about those areas where evangelicals do not agree? Should we throw up our hands in despair and say, "It's all a mystery, we can't know anything for sure about the future"? Unfortunately, far too many have done just that and others are doing it. No good is really accomplished by such an attitude, and such neglect of divine teaching cannot be pleasing to the Lord.

I suggest we take it as a challenge to study the Bible carefully and seek to understand as the Spirit teaches us what God wants us to know about the future. No book of the Bible is a closed book. Some have felt this way about the books of Daniel and Revelation. That is so unfortunate! God gave His Word to us so that we might know Him, His will, and His ways. God wants us to understand His Word; otherwise, there would have been little point in giving it to us and preserving it for us.

The Holy Spirit is the divine teacher for every child of God. He, Christ promised, will lead His own into all truth (John 16:13,14). Each believer has received God's Holy Spirit so that he might "know the things that are freely given to us of God" (I Corinthians 2:12). He teaches us, though, from the written Word of God. As we prayerfully study the Scriptures therefore, the Spirit will take what God has revealed and make it real to us. All who have been born again "have an unction from the Holy One" (I John 2:20). The "anointing" of the Spirit is the portion of every child of God (I John 2:27).

God has gifted men and given them to the church. We should avail ourselves of the fruit of their labors. There are many books available which present the various views of unfulfilled prophecy. After God's Word has been studied, it will be helpful to see how others understand it and how they have used it, or even misused it, in their system. A bibliography of select volumes, briefly annotated, have been included in this book to lend assistance in the understanding of the various views from those who embrace them.

Hold Convictions in Love

We can be sure God has a plan which will be carried out in the fulfillment of prophecy. He wants His people to believe and study His Word, all of it, so they will know what it teaches and fashion their lives accordingly. What one believes about last things matters and it matters mighty much. Other truths are affected by that belief. It is right to have and to hold definite beliefs about the future.

What is wrong, and seems to be rather prevalent, is the affirmation of our views in ways which are not Christlike. We may be one hundred per cent correct in what we believe, but if we do not hold those views in humility and with genuine Christian love for other believers who differ with us, we have sinned. It is not always easy, but our goal ought always be to speak the truth as we understand it, in love (Ephesians 4:15).

Evangelicals believe the whole Bible. They believe everything it teaches to be true. And yet having said that in all honesty, we must add, "But there are some things in Scripture which we hold with more certainty than other things." For example, we can be altogether certain the Bible teaches that Jesus Christ will come again to this earth. But we might not be nearly as certain about the identity of the twenty-four elders of Revelation 4:4 or of the man of sin of II Thessalonians 2:3. Then can we not display more humility, patience, and tolerance toward others and their viewpoints in these areas where Scripture is not clear or definitive? Let's hold our views and share our differences as fellow members of the family of God. Let's not suspect people of being less than orthodox just because they don't subscribe to the viewpoint on prophecy which we have been taught and believe. This is what I mean when I say, "Let's take prophecy out of the ring."

It is not wrong for churches, schools, and other organizations to have clearly stated specific views regarding the future. These institutions have a right to expect those associated with them to hold the same view. Neither should there be a halt to prophecy conferences and the publication of books and other literature in defense of a particular view of things to come.

By no means do I hope for, nor am I calling for a

scrapping of all attempts to outline the order of events in the future. Scripture does go beyond the general teachings of Christ's second coming, a future resurrection and judgment, and eternity to come. There are a significantly large number of passages which must be harmonized, related, and reconciled with these broad teachings. It is the believer's responsibility to rightly divide the Word of truth.

The church has always grown and prospered more through proliferation than it has through attempts of external unity. "The creative forces of the Christian faith have been unleashed not by unity but by proliferation . . . Unity is, in fact, not a healthy condition for a religious faith . . . The great spiritual movements of mankind have not been uniting movements but proliferating movements. Proliferation is the sign of life and health."[1]

The above words written with respect to the modern liberal attempt to build a world church are also applicable to the issues discussed in this book. The need is not for all views of eschatology to somehow be amalgamated into one broad all-inclusive belief. No, the differences need not be damaging. They can provide stimulation and vigor, providing those who hold them do so in a God-honoring way.

I am calling for an honest attempt to be more Christian over our differences. Let us speak the truth but let's be sure it is the truth. And then let's be doubly sure we speak it in that fruit of the Spirit, which is love.

Scripture does tell us to fight, but not over prophecy. Paul told Timothy to fight the good fight of the faith (I Timothy 6:12). And that is a responsbility which every believer has. Specifics of unfulfilled prophecy though can hardly be called essentials of the faith once delivered to the saints. We, like Timothy, are all to keep the faith (II Timothy 4:7). "The faith" surely cannot be construed to mean a particular order of future events. Yes, we are to do battle for God with the armor He provides (Ephesians

6:13-18). But the battle is to be against sin, Satan, and all the forces of evil including the religious forces.

Evangelicals have so much in common. It is such a shame that we so often fight each other instead of our real enemies. Some seem more willing to oppose and attack a brother who has a slightly different view of things to come than they are those who deny the faith (II Peter 2:1; II Corinthians 11:13-15). They are often more willing to join hands for some Christian cause with those who deny the faith than they are with other evangelicals who are not aligned with their view of future things.

There are those evangelicals who believe as long as one holds to their particular view of eschatology, all other doctrinal matters will somehow be in line. Their particular kind of eschatology is almost made a cure-all for other ills and a preventative of any future departures from the faith.

Evangelicals who have strong convictions about things to come need desperately to keep their views in proper perspective. I number myself among these. We need to exert ourselves against the real enemy of our souls and of the faith once delivered to the saints. God give us courage to have and to hold convictions concerning the future. May He also give us humility, patience, and love toward those who have not seen the light as we have.

SUGGESTIONS FOR ACTION

A group of children in rural Japan are said to meet their difficulties in a way which could be very helpful to evangelicals with differing views of unfulfilled prophecy.

Pillow education it might be called. Whenever the child has a difficulty or difference with another child, he is taught to sit on one side of a pillow. His hand is placed on it and he says, "I am all right and my friend is all wrong." Then he moves to another side of the pillow, places his hands on it, and says, "My friend is right and I am wrong." Next he moves to the third side, places his hands on the pillow and says, "Both my friend and I are wrong and both of us are right." Finally, the child moves to the fourth side of the pillow, places his hands on it, and often in deep thought says, "I am partly right and my friend is partly right."

All the positions evangelicals hold on unfulfilled prophecy have strengths and weaknesses. No one view is all right and all the others all wrong. As we allow the Holy Spirit to teach us through the Word, we must embrace that view which we feel is taught in Scripture and has the fewest and least bothersome problems.

What can be done in a practical way about the fight over the future? Are there any definite steps we can take which will help eliminate the fighting? I believe there are. It will do little good to read a book like this and be reminded of the facts of the fight unless we are motivated to take definite action toward removing the unnecessary friction and easing the conflict. These things apply to professionals and nonprofessionals alike.

Take Positive Action

There are certain positive actions which all of us as evangelical Christians can, and should, take, if we are determined to take prophecy out of the ring.

1. Determine to understand opposing views better and why they are held.

2. Determine to be less caustic about other evangelicals and their views.

3. Determine not to suspect a person's orthodoxy because he doesn't agree with us.

4. Determine to cooperate and fellowship whenever and wherever possible with those evangelicals who hold different views of unfulfilled prophecy.

Some Negative Action Needed

Some negative action also can go a long way toward bringing about positive results.

1. Avoid majoring on minors.

2. Avoid unwarranted dogmatism and conclusions.

3. Avoid a holier-than-thou attitude.

4. Avoid giving the impression that we have all the answers and others have all the problems.

5. Avoid thinking a view must be without any problems or it can't be right.

An epithet appears in a Latin treatise designed to uphold Lutheranism and at the same time calls for peace in that church. Reportedly, this treatise was published in Germany some time between 1615 and 1630. The message of the epithet is most fitting for our day too, especially in regard to the prophecy fight. I can't think of a better suggestion for action with regard to our attempt to understand the future than this.

Translated into English it reads:

In essentials unity,
In uncertainties freedom,
In all things love.

NOTES FOR CHAPTER 7

[1]C. Stanley Lowell, *The Ecumenical Mirage* (Grand Rapids: Baker Book House, 1967), pp. 65,76.

Selected Bibliography

A. Amillennialism

Adams, Jay. *The Time Is at Hand.* (Philadelphia: Presbyterian & Reformed Publishing Company, 1974. 123 pp.) Presentation of positive statement of the amillennial position as an orderly system.

Allis, O.T. *Prophecy and the Church.* (Philadelphia: Presbyterian & Reformed Publishing Company, 1945. 339 pp.) An examination and rejection of the dispensationalists' claim that the church is a mystery and that the Old Testament promises to Israel are fulfilled by the church.

Cox, William E. *Amillennialism Today.* (Philadelphia: Presbyterian & Reformed Publishing Company, 1966. 143 pp.) Presents the amillennial view of crucial doctrines related to eschatology.

Hamilton, Floyd E. *The Basis of Millennial Faith.* Grand Rapids: Wm. B. Eerdmans Publishing Company, 1942. 160 pp.) An attempt to present amillennialism as a system of belief and to show it is orthodox.

B. Postmillennialism

Boettner, Loraine. *The Millennium.* (Philadelphia: Presbyterian & Reformed Publishing Company, 1964. 380 pp.) Postmillennialism, amillennialism, and premillennialism are presented. Author argues in favor of postmillennialism.

Kik, J. Marcellus. *Matthew Twenty-Four* and *Revelation Twenty.* (Philadelphia: Presbyterian & Reformed Publishing Company, 1948, 1955 respectively. 97 pp and 92 pp respectively.) In these two books the author argues for postmillennialism from these crucial passages.

C. Premillennialism

Fineberg, Charles L. *Premillennialism or Amillennialism?* (Wheaton: VanKampen Press, 1954. 354 pp.) Both systems are compared and contrasted. Author argues for premillennialism.

McClain, Alva J. *The Greatness of the Kingdom.* (Chicago: Moody Press, 1968. 556 pp.) Traces idea of mediatorial kingdom through the Bible. Places strong emphasis upon premillennialism.

Pentecost, J. Dwight. *Things To Come.* (Grand Rapids: Zondervan Publishing Company, 1958. 633 pp.) Most complete presentation of premillennial pretribulational eschatology. Presents opposing views with author's refutations.

Ryrie, Charles C. *The Basis of Premillennial Faith.* (New York: Loizeaux Brothers, 1953. 160 pp.) Well outlined defense of premillennialism.

Walvoord, John F. *The Millennial Kingdom.* (Findlay, Ohio: Dunham Publishing Company, 1959. 373 pp.) Comprehensive treatment of the millennial systems. Author builds case for premillennialism from Scripture and history.

D. Midtribulationism

Harrison, Norman B. *The End.* (Minneapolis, Minnesota: Harrison Service, 1941. 239 pp.) Defense for the rapture in the middle of Daniel's seventieth week.

E. Partial Rapturism

Brubaker, Ray. *The Purpose of the Great Tribulation.* (St. Petersburg, Florida, 1968. 8 pp. and other pamphlets.) Viewing one of the purposes of the tribulation as a means of testing lukewarm Christians the author argues his case for partial rapturism.

Lang, G. H. *The Revelation of Jesus Christ.* (London: Oliphants, 1945. 420 pp.) Most complete and comprehensive presentation of the partial rapture position available.

F. Posttribulationism

Gundry, Robert H. *The Church and the Tribulation.* (Grand Rapids: Zondervan Publishing Company, 1973. 224 pp.) Most recent and exegetically based defense of premillennial posttribulationism. Author seeks to build his case by showing that passages often used in defense of pretribulationalism may also be used to support posttribulationism.

Ladd, George E. *That Blessed Hope.* (Grand Rapids: Zondervan

Publishing Company, 1956, 167 pp.) Defines the blessed hope not as deliverance from the tribulation but preservation through it. A premillennial posttribulational defense.

Payne, J. Barton. *The Imminent Appearing of Christ.* (Grand Rapids: Wm. B. Eerdmans Publishing Co., 1962. 191 pp.) Presents a new view of imminency which the author feels is in harmony with posttribulationism.

Reese, Alexander. *The Approaching Advent of Christ.* (London: Marshall, Morgan, & Scott, [n.d.], 328 pp.) A classic posttribulational polemic.

G. Pretribulationism

English, E. Schuyler. *Re-Thinking the Rapture.* (Travelers Rest, South Carolina: Southern Bible Book House, 1954. 123 pp.) Brief and concise defense of pretribulationism.

Walvoord, John F. *The Rapture Question.* (Grand Rapids: Zondervan Publishing Company, 1957. 204 pp.) The various views respecting the time of the rapture and the participants in it are presented. Author sets forth arguments used in defense of the positions and concludes by giving fifty arguments for pretribulationism.

Wood, Leon J. *Is the Rapture Next?* (Grand Rapids: Zondervan Publishing Company, 1956. 120 pp.) A solid defense of pretribulationism. The crucial issues are all dealt with.

H. Anti-dispensationalism

Bass, Clarence B. *Backgrounds to Dispensationalism.* (Grand Rapids: Wm. B. Eerdmans Publishing Company, 1960. 184 pp.) An attempted refutation of the dispensational system by appealing to its recency and by showing flaws in one of the earlier spokesmen for the system.

Cox, William E. *An Examination of Dispensationalism.* (Philadelphia: Presbyterian & Reformed Publishing Company, 1963. 61 pp.) Author finds problems with dispensational beliefs and with early spokesmen of the view.

Kraus, C. Norma. *Dispensationalism in America.* (Richmond, Virginia: John Knox Press, 1958. 156 pp.) Deals with rise of dispensationalism and with relation of dispensationalism to premillennialism.

I. Dispensationalism

Barndollar, Walker W. *The Validity of Dispensationalism.* (Des Plaines, Illinois: Regular Baptist Press, 1964. 47 pp.) Shows the logic and Biblical base for dispensationalism.

Chafer, Lewis Sperry. *Dispensations.* (Dallas: Dallas Theological Seminary Press, 1936. 108 pp.) In this volume the founder of Dallas Theological Seminary presents a brief statement of the relation of dispensationalism to other vital doctrines.

Ryrie, Charles C. *Dispensationalism Today.* (Chicago: Moody Press, 1965. 221 pp.) This is a complete and contemporary presentation of dispensationalism as a system of theology.

J. Biblical Interpretation

Ramm, Bernard. *Protestant Biblical Interpretation.* (Boston: W. A. Wilde Company, 1950. 197 pp.) A standard text on the interpretation of Scripture in general.

Tan, Paul Lee. *The Interpretation of Prophecy.* (Winona Lake, Indiana: B. M. H. Books, Inc., 1974. 435 pp.) A detailed defense for the literal interpretation of prophecy.

**MEDITATION THAT
TRANSCENDS
By Robert P. Lightner**

Transcendental Meditation is sweeping
the country. Dr. Lightner examines the TM
phenomenon from a Christian point of view
in a scripturally documented, easily
read little book that every Christian
will want to read. Paper **$.95**

ACCENT BOOKS
Denver, Colorado